"I try to relate [illegible] rs, Uber drivers, and stu[illegible] t so far. *Islam and North* [illegible], understanding, and lo[illegible] hopefulness, wisdom, an[illegible] perspectives of these authors."

—**Linda Bergquist**, church planting catalyst, North American Mission Board

"The authors of *Islam and North America* have not only read about Islam; they have lived intentionally to minister to Muslims in North America and around the world. This book is the product of their wisdom and experience and will serve anyone who wants to reach those in their community. As we gain a better understanding of this important group, my prayer is that a growing number of believers will befriend and share the gospel with their Muslim neighbors."

—**Kevin Ezell**, president, North American Mission Board

"The peoples of Islam comprise the most promising mission field in the world today, and those who want to be on the front lines of God's greatest work will be engaging with Muslims. As Micah Fries and Keith Whitfield show us, God has brought the front lines to our back door. They have compiled some of our generation's brightest evangelical minds to show us how we can effectively [engage] with them. This is an insightful and helpful work at an opportune time. I am excited to commend it."

—**J. D. Greear**, president, Southern Baptist Convention, and pastor, The Summit Church, Raleigh-Durham, NC

"The Great Commandment is easy to assent to but difficult to live out, especially in our rapidly changing communities. Micah Fries and Keith Whitfield have provided a timely, helpful, and practical book on how to love some of our least known North American neighbors, Muslims. They have done a masterful job of assembling scholars, practitioners, and multiple former Muslims to help us get to better know our Muslim neighbors in order to meaningfully love them."

—**Greg Mathias**, assistant professor of global studies, associate director, Center for Great Commission Studies, Southeastern Baptist Theological Seminary

"The Christian encounter with Islam is one of the most pressing realities faced by the church today. Micah Fries and Keith Whitfield bring together much-needed resources in this single volume—combining pastoral insight and scholarship. This book is a timely contribution that will greatly serve Christian leaders and congregations."

—**R. Albert Mohler Jr.**, president, The Southern Baptist Theological Seminary

"God is moving in the twenty-first century to fulfill his mission in unprecedented ways. The gospel is penetrating previously unreached people groups, and church growth is accelerating around the world. The world of Islam seems to be the remaining formidable barrier for fulfilling the Great Commission. Yet God, as sovereign over the nations, is moving in amazing ways in using globalization, persecution, and political disruption to bring masses of Muslims to America. *Islam and North America* is a valuable tool to help churches and individual Christians understand Islam and how to reach them for Christ in the new sociological context of our own community. Written by an array of seasoned missiologists, and those with cross-cultural witnessing experience, this book will equip Christians to build relationships and seize the privilege of extending the kingdom of God to those long resistant to the gospel."

—**Jerry Rankin**, president emeritus, International Mission Board, senior fellow, Zwemer Center for Muslim Studies

Micah Fries | Keith Whitfield

ISLAM AND NORTH AMERICA

Loving our Muslim Neighbors

NASHVILLE, TENNESSEE

Islam and North America

Published by B&H Academic
Nashville, Tennessee

ISBN: 978-1-4627-4841-9

DEWEY: 297
SUBHD: ISLAM \ MUSLIMS \ ISLAMIC AMERICANS

Printed in the United States of America

1 2 3 4 5 6 7 8 9 10 VP 23 22 21 20 19 18

To our parents,
Paul and Cheryl Fries
and
Larry and Cheryl Whitfield

For teaching us to love Jesus and the nations
for the glory of God and his great name.

CONTENTS

PART 3: GREAT COMMISSION OPPORTUNITIES

FOREWORD
A CALL TO KEEP GOING
Kambiz Saghaey

In 1997, on the island of Cyprus in the Mediterranean Sea, an angry man entered an evangelical church. This small church, started by international missionaries, was baptizing former Muslims. The man who entered the church door that day was raised as a devout Iranian Muslim. He chanted the Quran in public competitions and performed the call to prayer. He came that day to challenge the leadership of the church for converting Muslims to Christianity.

For the next nine months, this man argued with the church members about the tenets of Christianity, causing many problems for them. Someone gave him a Bible to read, and he ignored it because he believed the Bible was full of errors. But his wife suggested that they should read the Bible so they could better argue with the Christians. The more they read the Bible, however, the more they began to question Islam.

My name is Kambiz, and that angry Islamic man was me.

As I read the Bible and argued with those Christians, I came to the point where I didn't even know who I was anymore. My heart began to change. While I was still angry with God, I began praying. For three weeks, this was my prayer to God: "For twenty-seven years

I did my best. I followed the sharia law to the letter. I did all the things you told me to do, and now you tell me the things I believe are wrong? I will follow you. I want to worship you, but I need to see you! Won't you come down and show yourself to me?" Then one day, as I sat in a church service, still wondering about this question, the text of John 3:7–8 caused new thoughts to flood into my mind. This passage talks about how we don't know where the wind comes from. God said to me, "You want to see me? I have come. I am inside you." I sensed God's presence during that worship service, and I gave my heart to the Lord. My wife, Sepideh, was in church also, and I went to her and told her that I had given my heart to the Lord. "I'm so happy," she said. "Last week it happened to me too. I was praying for you."

God used two things in particular to change my heart. The first one was the display of love among the church members. One example of this love was when one of them brought his motorcycle to our house on Sunday. The man knew we did not have a ride to church, so he left his motorcycle for me and my family to use, and he walked thirty minutes to church. At first, I thought the people were planning to deceive me with false acts of love. But later on, I realized that this love was sincere, and it came from their hearts. Finding this pure sort of love outside of church was impossible. The second thing God used to change me was the way these Christians answered life's hard questions. Muslims answer religious questions with stories; Christians can give answers about life's most important questions directly from the Bible.

Life as Disciples of Jesus

In 2000, Sepideh and I moved to Istanbul, Turkey, and we started a house church there. Then, in 2003, we felt called by God to return to Iran despite the harsh treatment of Christians by the Iranian authorities. Witnessing to Muslims is forbidden in Iran, and those who leave Islam face the death penalty. The authorities there often raid house-church services and arrest those in attendance. The smuggling in, publishing, or reprinting of Bibles and Christian literature is illegal. In spite of this anti-Christian environment, however, I pastored my first Iranian house church in 2003. We started out with only two members: my wife and me. But God richly blessed our underground church by multiplying the believers. Before long, our one little congregation had become three churches with seventy members total, and I was their pastor.

God commands all believers in Matt 28:19 to "go, therefore, and make disciples." Therefore, our underground churches started ministering to a nomadic people group. These nomads had no electricity, and they could not read or write. So the only way to share the gospel with them was to set up a tent among them. This is what we did. For seven years, these churches served Jesus without detection.

Praising God in Jail

I had always expected to be arrested in Iran for pastoring underground house churches. Seven years after starting my first church, my time finally came. While we were celebrating an early Christmas party on December 15, 2009, more than twenty Iranian policemen stormed through the front door of the house in which we were meeting. Everyone's personal information and cell phones were collected. For six months, there had been a spy in the midst of our congregation, and I had become a target of the authorities.

That evening, just ten days before Christmas, I found myself in a jail cell. I was blindfolded and intensely questioned regarding my involvement in the three local house churches. At first, my heart and mind raced, worrying about my family, the churches, and the future. But then God reminded me of how he had brought me through other challenges in my life. I experienced a deep peace as I remembered that God was still in control. After that, one of the main things I did while I was in jail was give praise to him.

Sepideh and our two young children had no idea where I was for twenty-one days. They simply but fearfully thought I was missing until three weeks later, when they learned where I was being held by the authorities. However, my future still wasn't certain. The corrupt practices of the Iranian prison meant that I wasn't officially registered as a prisoner. This meant that anything could happen to me—including death—and no one would know. Finally, after more than two months behind bars, I was registered as an official prisoner.

The interrogator tried many tactics to learn more about the network of underground Christians and their nearby house churches. One day he would shout in my face; the next day he would offer me money and goods if I would agree to return to Islam. He even tried to use my adopted daughter to leverage my cooperation, threatening to remove her from our home if I did not help. Psychologically, it was very hard. I expected that at any time they would begin to beat me.

Finding Freedom

After eighty-six days in jail, a friend posted my bail of $45,000, and I was released. It was then that I learned about the spy who had been attending one of our house churches and had informed the government officials of these "subversive" Christian gatherings. Because of this, I faced two charges: one for subverting the Iranian government, and the other for subverting Islam. In Iran, we have a two-court system: the Revolutionary Court and the civil court. The charges of subverting the government were to be heard by the Revolutionary Court, and the charges of subverting Islam were to be heard by the civil court.

First, I was tried for subverting the government. As I prepared for my case in the Revolutionary Court, Sepideh shared her faith with the prosecutor and told him the church was fasting and praying for him.

"Really? For me?" the prosecutor said.

"Yes, for you, because of the position you're in," Sepideh said. "It is God's job to judge. But God gave that position to you."

The judge in the Revolutionary Court found nothing against me based on the original charges. He pointed out that I hadn't done anything against the government; rather, I was a Muslim who had simply become a Christian, and for that reason, the judge wanted to change the charge to apostasy. When he couldn't change the charges, he looked at me and told me: "I will find something against you to kill you." I was released, but when I went back to court, the prosecutor took my case before another judge, who acquitted me of all charges, with a time of probation. I later found out that the reason we changed courts was that the judge who'd threatened me had died. Everyone knew my wife and I were praying for the court officials. Now, the legal authorities now feared us.

During those times, Ps 37:32, 36 was very real in my life. The passage says, "The wicked one lies in wait for the righteous and seeks to kill him. . . . Then I passed by and noticed he was gone; I searched for him, but he could not be found." The prosecutor whom we had prayed for previously asked me if I had also prayed for the judge who died. I told him, yes, we had prayed—we prayed for his healing, not for his death. But his death was God's decision, and God's will was done.

This situation shows the Lord's power to protect his children by saving me from death, but the judge in the civil case found me guilty and sentenced me to two years in prison. After several unsuccessful appeals, my family and I moved to Turkey and applied for asylum with the United Nations as refugees.

Continuing God's Work

We spent the next four years in Turkey, where we started two new churches for Iranian believers and launched a training center for Iranian pastors. These churches conduct outreach programs for Iranian tourists, including during the time of Nowruz, which marks the Iranian New Year. Each March, 2 million Iranians celebrate this holiday in Turkey. Last year alone, our churches partnered with other churches to distribute Christian literature to about 7,600 Muslims in Istanbul.

While in Turkey, I took Southeastern Seminary classes through their distance learning program. About a year ago, our family moved to the United States. Sepideh and I are now both studying on-campus at Southeastern Baptist Theological Seminary in Wake Forest, North Carolina, and we work among Iranian students, businesspeople, and refugees. Before we came to Southeastern, Lexington Baptist Church in Lexington, South Carolina, helped our family settle into the United States. Our relationship with that church started while we were in Turkey, when some of its members traveled overseas to partner with us in ministry.

I am so glad God gave me this opportunity. I am thankful to have the freedom to study the Bible and worship God.

I also preach online to Iranian churches in Turkey, and Sepideh writes radio programs to reach more Iranians for Christ. Recently, I became coordinator for Persian leadership development at Southeastern Seminary. My vision in this new position is to start high school, college, and seminary programs online in the Farsi language, for Christians both in Iran and outside the country. We do these things because the people in this region of the world are in desperate need of the gospel.

In Iran today, there is great persecution of Christians. This current wave of persecution began during the Islamic Revolution under the reign of Ruhollah Khomeini, the grand ayatollah. Yet paradoxically, I believe that the ayatollah is responsible for the tremendous growth of Christianity in Iran. He so strongly emphasized Islam that people have seen its true face—and many are turning back from it as a result. In 1979, there were relatively few Christians in Iran. Today, as many as 2 million believers may be living within its borders. I foresee the Iranian church continuing its rapid growth in the next few decades. Iran is the first country in the region that is turning to Christianity.

In my online messages to some of the Iranian believers, I explain to them that persecution is part of the Christian faith. Some people complain about the persecution, but these circumstances are meant to bring us closer to God. Persecution is a test of our faith. And if this testing doesn't come, how will we know our faith is actually real?

The opportunity my family now has to study and worship God freely is allowing us to help young Farsi-speaking churches grow. These churches are growing quickly but not deeply. To live out the gospel, they need strong roots in the faith.

Christ has called me to "go and make disciples" (Matt 28:19 NIV). He has given me a vision to witness for him "in Jerusalem, and in all Judea and Samaria, and to the ends of the earth" (Acts 1:8 NIV). My "Jerusalem" is the Raleigh area in North Carolina, where there are more than 8,000 Persian speakers. I desire to teach their churches how to reach Muslims with the gospel. My "Judea" is those Iranian churches in Virginia and Georgia that are weak and need strengthening in the faith. "Samaria," for me, consists of the refugees in Turkey, Malaysia, and Germany who need discipleship and leadership training. And to "the ends of the earth" in Iran, I need to produce training videos and send these materials to believers inside the country.

I believe that the Lord's words to "go and make disciples" are not just for building up churches but are for individual believers too. There is no other choice, because this is God's command for us. The underground church should pursue this mission, and the believers in free countries should do the same.

Just as those church members in Cyprus shared their faith with me, we should all share our faith with others. All members of every church are missionaries, sent by the Lord Jesus to share their faith with their neighbors. If we all obey this commission from the Lord, God will give his blessing, and God will grow his church. I hope this book helps you to obey this commission by loving your Muslim neighbors and sharing the good news with them.

ACKNOWLEDGMENTS AND INTRODUCTION

This book is a labor "motivated by love" (1 Thess 1:3 AMP). It is easy to love those who are most like us, but it is distinctively Christian to love those who are least like us. To be like Jesus means to love those who are often opposed to us or, at a minimum, who profoundly disagree with us. When Jesus redeems us from sin and death, he compels us to become like him, and he sends us on mission to proclaim the gospel to all people everywhere. We worked on this book from our shared conviction that as members of the human race, we are all deeply broken, that the grace of Jesus alone is what redeems us, and that the One who redeemed us desires all people to be redeemed (1 Tim 2:4).

We invite you to read this book as a pursuit of learning to love. We pray that this book will help you love the world and everyone in it. Every person on the planet is created by God and bears his image. Each one is deeply precious to him. Even more directly, we want this book to help us love a group of people who come from a different culture and follow a different religion than we do.

Islam and North America prepares the church to know and love our Muslim friends and neighbors, and to help you learn how to personally declare and display the gospel of Jesus to them. It will guide you to see the Great Commission opportunities provided by

Muslim migration to North America. We will also introduce you to the trends and patterns of Islam's growth in North America and help you prepare for the emerging missional opportunities.

We did not start this project because we believed that we have something to say, but because we believe that something needed to be said. We are grateful that B&H Academic saw the value of this project. In particular, Chris Thompson and Audrey Greeson, our editors at B&H Academic, have guided this book through the publication process, being supportive and encouraging partners in this work. Beth Holmes, Meredith Cook, Josh Alley, Owen Kelly, and Blair Smith also helped us prepare the manuscript for publication, offering careful proofreading and insightful comments that made the book better.

We invited a group of people to write chapters who do have something to teach us about Islam and how to reach its followers. Leaders in missions and cross-cultural engagement are present in these pages. Religious leaders who have engaged Muslims throughout the world and have led Christians to engage in multiethnic conversations, as well as a number of former Muslims, contributed chapters to this book. We are thankful for all those who agreed to add their insights to this work. We asked them to join in this venture to help equip the church for the Great Commission opportunities that the recent growth in Muslim immigration has created for us.

Change is often imperceptible; we typically discern that change has taken place only after some time passes. The growth in the Muslim population in North America is noticeable—it has happened relatively quickly. And it is unsettling for many people, including Christians. The church in North America needs some guidance when it comes to engaging Muslims with the gospel. We are concerned that fear, which opposes the explicit commands of Jesus, is controlling many in the church. This means that the church does not look like Jesus. The presence of this fear may cause us to miss an opportunity to share the gospel of Jesus Christ with our Muslim friends and neighbors. Our goal is for this book to alleviate some unfounded concerns and encourage us as Christians to let love overcome legitimate concerns so that we might be available to engage the newcomers next door.

When it comes to Islam, our national apprehension is exacerbated by the profound religious and cultural differences and by the suspicion of threat. It does appear that there has been an increase of terrorist activity on United States soil since 2013. Boston, Massachusetts. Fort Hood, Texas. Chattanooga, Tennessee. San Bernardino, California. And as we finalized the manuscript for this book, New York, New York, on October 31, 2017. During this same period, in Europe we have seen terrorist attacks in Paris as well as in Brussels, Wurzburg, Berlin, Westminster, London, Stockholm, Manchester, and Barcelona. In July 2017, *Christianity Today* published an article that reported that two-thirds of white evangelicals "believe Islam is not part of mainstream American society," and nearly 75 percent consider there to be "a natural conflict between Islam and democracy." The reason they gave for their beliefs is that Islam encourages violence more than other faiths.[1]

Current events remind us not only that we control so very little of what takes place around us, but that there are people who have been shaped by ideas and beliefs that are dangerous to a safe and peaceful society. While these statements are true in general, they certainly ring true about events carried out on North American soil since 9/11. These events have only heightened people's fears. We observed this in the public debate around immigration in the 2016 presidential election and in people's response to the January 2017

[1] Kate Shellnutt, "Most White Evangelicals Don't Believe Muslims Belong in America," *Christianity Today*, July 26, 2017, http://www.christianitytoday.com/news/2017/july/pew-how-white-evangelicals-view-us-muslims-islam.html.

executive order pertaining to immigrants, refugees, and protection against terrorism.

In light of this reality, we need to break the ice when it comes to encouraging Christians to consider the Great Commission opportunities. We have to reach Muslims in our own communities. This is an icebreaker kind of book.

The idea for the book came from conversations with family, friends, neighbors, and strangers. Fear was hinted at—and sometimes even explicitly expressed—in those conversations. We believed that a book was needed to help people think through the present cultural anxiety.

We are not trying to negotiate immigration policy in these pages. That is an important discussion, but a discussion for another time. Miguel Echevarria has contributed an afterword for this book that addresses immigration from a biblical perspective. This essay helps Christians see the providential, missional opportunity immigration provides us. It does not deal with all the difficult public-policy considerations.

What we are trying to do is help you get a sense of what is actually happening within the Muslim community in North America. To some extent, we are trying to calm your fears by offering you facts, data, and personal stories, not to mention biblical truth, that pulls away the hysteria and reveals the danger of false narratives. In another sense, we are saying that, regardless of what threats we may face, "even if you should suffer for righteousness, you are blessed" (1 Pet 3:14). We are trying to help you see the opportunities that the church currently has to reach unreached peoples. We are trying to establish your convictions. We are trying to prepare you to engage.

In the first chapter, Ed Stetzer introduces us to the realities, challenges, and opportunities of living in a multi-faith world. He reminds us that the multiplicity of faiths provides a context for people to share the uniqueness of their various religions. Stetzer provides four principles that orient the tone, content, and instruction for the rest of this book. He cautions believers against leaping too quickly to conclusions about the beliefs of their Muslim neighbors. He urges Christians instead to initiate real dialogue with their Muslim neighbors in order to truly engage them with, and freely offer them, the gospel.

Steve A. Johnson follows up by describing the growth of Muslims in North America, predicting continued increase between now and 2050. He explains the immigration patterns of Muslims to the United States, their expression of culture and religion once they arrive, and the common social values that they hold with Christians. He also provides the distinctives and gives an overview of the various Islamic groups.

Chapters 3 through 7 answer questions that people are asking. Most of these chapters give you the opportunity to practice listening carefully to what Muslims believe and how that differs from Christianity. This material will help you talk more confidently with Muslims, not so you can dismiss their beliefs but so that you understand them better when they share their beliefs with you.

In chapter 3, C. Fyne Nsofor calls for dialogue with your Muslim neighbor that engages rather than ignores the real differences between Islam and Christianity. In chapter 4, Bart Barber speaks to why American Christians hesitate to support the rights of Muslims to practice Islam freely in the United States, but also argues that Christians undermine their own right to practice their faith when they do not support everyone's right to worship.

In chapter 5, Keith S. Whitfield picks up some of these themes to answer the question, "Do Christians and Muslims worship the same God?" He does this by establishing the key trinitarian distinctives of the Christian faith and explaining a strategy for discussing the Trinity with Muslims. Ayman Ibrahim tackles the difficult topic of Islam and jihad in chapter 6. He takes us on a journey through the Quran and the hadith to define jihad by Islam's sacred texts rather than by the actions of some Muslims. He also discusses the use of jihad in Arabic translations of the Bible, demonstrating that the call to violence within Islam is not as cut-and-dried as many of us would like to think. Bob Roberts closes out the second section of the book by addressing the difficult question of the Muslim political agenda, particularly relating to sharia law. He takes on many misconceptions Americans have concerning Muslims and sharia, and he shares some of the personal conversations he has had on this topic. The only way to understand what sharia means to your Muslim neighbor, he says, is to ask your Muslim neighbor.

In the final section of the book, we seek to prepare you for the Great Commission opportunities that arise when Muslims live in your community. Micah Fries reminds us in chapter 8 that immigration opens immigrants to new possibilities, and often immigrants are open to consider new patterns of life and explore new worldviews as well. He encourages Christians to build real friendships with Muslim immigrants, for these friendships tend to lead to gospel conversations. In chapter 9, D. A. Horton suggests practical ways to get to know your Muslim neighbors. He addresses the barriers that arise between Christians and non-Christians and suggests that genuine compassion is the key to overcome those barriers.

Shirin Taber and Ant Greenham (chapters 10 and 11) both explain why genuine love and relationships open gospel doors when Christians desire to engage Muslims. Taber tells about her experience of living in the United States as a young Iranian woman and urges us to pursue our Muslim neighbors through self-giving love in order to tear down the stereotypes that so often impact these relationships. Greenham examines the communal nature of Islamic culture and shows how important Christian community is in drawing Muslims to the gospel.

In the last chapter of the book, Afshin Ziafat prepares us for gospel conversations with Muslims. He discusses the difference between Christian and Muslim beliefs regarding God, man, Jesus, and salvation. Sharing the gospel with a Muslim requires believers to address these issues, Ziafat says, so he gives helpful guidance for Christians in this endeavor.

We pray this book will help you see the opportunities you have to reach people from different cultures in North America. May God grant those of you who bear the name of Jesus that conviction to stand together and radically love your Muslim neighbors. Show them the gospel of grace in how you live the gospel truth faithfully. Declare to them how the gospel that saves sinners can save them. Teach them that God requires their faith only, and he will give them grace abundantly.

We leave you with Jesus's words: "Love the Lord your God with all your heart, with all your soul, and with all your mind. This is the greatest and most important command. The second is like it: Love your neighbor as yourself" (Matt 22:37–39).

PART 1

OVERVIEW OF ISLAM IN NORTH AMERICA

1

Islam, North America, and the New Multi-Faith Reality: How Now Shall We Live?[1]

Ed Stetzer

In 1985, when a mosque opened in Elizabethtown, Kentucky, more than a few eyebrows were raised. Elizabethtown had a large Islamic population, and those Muslims supported the construction of a mosque and Islamic cultural center. Today, it still stands. And though the current imam is not a Muslim immigrant (he is from Ann Arbor, Michigan), this quintessential American small town is host to a growing Islamic community.

If you travel over to the eastern part of Kentucky, you will find the coal-mining town of Prestonsburg, where I went on my first mission trip. At that time, the little Episcopal church we worked with seemed like the odd one out among the Pentecostals and Baptists. Now, if you travel a few miles outside of Prestonsburg, you will find an elegant mosque

[1] This chapter is adapted from a previously published article. See Ed Stetzer, "Proselytizing in a Multi-Faith World," *Christianity Today*, March 28, 2011, http://www.christianitytoday.com/ct/2011/april/proselytizingmultifaith.html.

tucked away in a narrow hollow.[2] Appalachia, long a home to poor coal-mining communities, is now host to a growing Islamic community.

We are in the midst of what the media have called the "Changing Face of America."[3] This transformation raises many questions. One foundational question is, what does it mean to be an American in the twenty-first century? Before 1965, most immigrants followed the WASP (White Anglo-Saxon Protestant) profile. For the majority of Americans, immigrants were like "us." They looked like "us," they learned "our" language, and they believed as "we" did. Since the Immigration Act of 1965, immigration has looked different. The newer waves of immigrants are not white, they are not Anglo-Saxon, and they certainly are not Protestant. America is becoming a nation of multiple cultures and multiple faiths.

A recent Pew Research study estimates that 3.3 million Muslims lived in America in 2015, and projects their population to grow to more than 8 million by 2050.[4] The actual numbers are difficult to determine because the data relies on Muslims in America who are willing to report. Many Islamic immigrants are reluctant to do so because of fear of discrimination. Their fear is not without reason, as half of the pastors in America view Islam as a dangerous religion that promotes violence.[5] These are the same pastors whose Bibles tell them to make disciples of all nations.

---

[2] Kevin Williams, "The Muslims of Appalachia: Kentucky Coal Country Embracing the Faithful," Aljazeera America, February 21, 2016, http://america.aljazeera.com/articles/2016/2/21/muslims-appalachia-kentucky.html.

[3] See, for example, "Changing Face of America: The Diversity Index Explained," *USA Today*, March 18, 2013, https://www.usatoday.com/videos/news/nation/2015/03/18/17657383/.

[4] Besheer Mohamed, "A New Estimate of the U.S. Muslim Population," Pew Research Center, January 6, 2016, http://www.pewresearch.org/fact-tank/2016/01/06/a-new-estimate-of-the-u-s-muslim-population.

[5] Ed Stetzer, "Perception of Islam among Protestant Pastors," *The Exchange* (blog), April 23, 2010, http://www.christianitytoday.com/edstetzer/2010/april/perceptions-of-islam-among-protestant-pastors.html.

The Christian church, in order to be faithful, must consider what it looks like to have a gospel witness in a country composed of many faiths. We believe the answer lies in learning to live in a multi-faith world.

Living in a Multi-Faith World

Some years ago, I attended an "interfaith" meeting in Chicago that hosted a number of Christian denominations as well as a variety of other faiths. The goal was to compare research findings on our respective faith communities. At one point I questioned if I belonged at the meeting. The facilitator explained that the research should lead to cooperative resourcing to help all faiths develop and grow. I did not sign up for that. At the appropriate time, and with my best smile, I raised my hand and said something like this: "I appreciate the funding that allows us to survey our churches, and I think it is helpful to use similar questions and metrics for better research. But I am not here to form a partnership to help one another. I want to help the churches I serve, and part of the reason they exist is to convert some of you." Some participants in the room looked at me as if I had just uttered a string of profanities. Others nodded in agreement. Then the Muslim imam seated next to me said, in effect, "I feel the same way."

Though the imam and I were minorities in that group of predominantly liberal Protestants, we represented the movements (evangelical and Muslim) within that meeting that were (and still are) actually growing in numbers. Both he and I believed in sharing our faiths and enlarging their reach. We did not think we were worshipping the same God or gods, and we were not there under the pretense that we held the same beliefs. In other words, our goal was not merging faiths, combining beliefs, or even interfaith partnership. We acknowledged that we were not of the same faith and that we would each be overjoyed if we could bring the other to the truth—not just our truth but *the* truth as we firmly believed it.

Without using the word, we were acknowledging that, in such a context, we in North America are *multi-faith*.

When people of different faiths are found together in a conference, neighborhood, or nation, they are best described as "multi-faith," representing different faiths. "Multi-faith" might sound strange to some, yet the idea is significant if peaceful coexistence and mutual understanding in a crowded religious world are important—and I think they are. The Christian witness in North America depends on it.

We are long past the day when Christianity is the privileged religious voice in North America. Evangelicals lamenting "the former days" is no way forward. The future of Christian witness is learning to live with multi-faith neighbors who are now in the city centers, the suburbs, and, yes, even rural America, and loving people of other faiths, engaging them with the Christian message.

Multi-Faith Living Is Not Interfaith Dialogue

For years, people of various faiths have promoted "interfaith dialogue" in order to discover common ground and work together for humanity's sake. That sounds good until we start digging below the surface.

Those involved in interfaith dialogue often approach it as if there are no fundamental distinctions between the faiths. By way of contrast, in a multi-faith world, we recognize that we are neither worshipping the same God or gods, nor pursuing the same goals. Furthermore, we are not offended by our mutual desire to proselytize one another. The central assumption among those in the interfaith dialogue business has traditionally been that, at their core, all religious people—Hindus and Buddhists, Muslims and Jews, Christians and animists—are striving for the same thing, and are just using different words and concepts to get there. We should therefore, the reasoning goes, be able to cooperate around common beliefs to improve society. But how true is that assumption?

This book is about a Christian missionary encounter with Islam in North America. So, the main focus is understanding Islam and how to engage it with the gospel. Nevertheless, to illustrate the importance of multi-faith interaction, let's take a closer look at the four religions that represent about three-quarters of the global population.

Recent surveys indicate that, worldwide, there are 2.1 billion Christians, 1.5 billion Muslims, 900 million Hindus, and 376 million Buddhists.[6] The most basic belief in each religion is the idea of God.

Within the various streams of Hindu thought alone, there are multiple answers to the question, who or what is god? Hindus may believe that there is one god, 330 million gods, or no god at all. The Vedas—the most ancient of Hindu scriptures, which are accepted by most Hindus as normative—teach that "atman is Brahman," or "the soul is god," meaning that god is in each of us and each of us is part of god. The common Hindu greeting "Namaste," which means, roughly, "The god within me recognizes and greets the god within you," reflects this belief.

In his apologetic for the Buddhist faith, Shravasti Dhammika, the author of several popular books on Buddhism, writes, "Do Buddhists believe in god? No, we do not. There are several reasons for this. The Buddha, like modern sociologists and psychologists, believed that religious ideas and especially the god idea, have their origin in fear. The Buddha says, 'Gripped by fear, men go to the sacred mountains, sacred groves, sacred trees and shrines.'"[7] So, for

[6] Adherents.com, "Major Religions of the World Ranked by Number of Adherents," accessed April 19, 2018, http://www.adherents.com/Religions_By_Adherents.html.

[7] Ven. S. Dhammika, *Good Question, Good Answer*, quoted in "Buddha and the God Idea," Buddha.net, accessed March 13, 2018, https://www.buddhanet.net/e-learning/qanda03.htm.

most orthodox Buddhists in the Theravada tradition, the concept of a personal, supreme being is at best unimportant and at worst an oppressive superstition. Mahayana Buddhism, a later development, has by contrast deified the Buddha and allows for his incarnations in especially worthy people who delay their eternal release—their nirvana—so that their accumulated merits may be transferred to their devotees. In other words, even Buddhism itself does not agree on the concept of God.

How is God conceived in Islam? In the Quran we read, "Say: He is Allah, the One and Only. Allah, the Eternal, Absolute. He begets not, nor is he begotten. And there is none like unto him" (QS 112:1–4). We find foundational Islamic beliefs about the character of Allah in this passage: He is unique. No other being is like him. He is sovereign over all things. He has always existed and will always exist. And he is the father to no one.

In contrast, Christians believe that there is one God, who is the Creator of the world. He is a personal God—a conscious, free, and righteous being. And he is not only a personal God but a God of providence who is involved in the day-to-day affairs of creation. He is a righteous God who expects ethical behavior from each of us. He expects his followers to live out their belief by loving him with all their hearts, souls, and minds, and by loving their neighbors as themselves (Matt 22:37–39). God, while one in essence, also reveals himself in three persons: Father, Son, and Holy Spirit.

So, according to the four largest world religions, God is either one with creation and takes on millions of forms, or God may or may not exist, or God is numerically one and absolute, or God is one but exists in three persons. If we cannot agree on even the basic definition of God or his character, how can we say that all the major religions are on the same path toward the truth about God? Pretending that we all believe the same thing does not foster dialogue but in fact prohibits it. We must acknowledge that humankind is, in fact, multi-faith—with radically different visions of the future, eternity, and the path to getting there.

Being a Neighbor

Admitting that humans are multi-faith is only a beginning. We also need to be willing to live together with those whose beliefs are different from our own. This means allowing adherents of other faiths to live out their convictions without creating constant conflict. The world has seen too much pain and suffering as the result of followers of one faith using political or military means to impose their views on followers of another. So how do religions that are mutually exclusive peacefully exist side by side?

In the spirit of multi-faith dialogue, I would like to propose four foundational commitments that Christians can make:

1. Let each religion speak for itself.
2. Talk with and about *individuals,* not generic "faiths."
3. Respect others who hold to different beliefs, just as you would expect them to respect you for yours.
4. Grant each person the freedom to make his or her faith decisions.

What would each of these look like in practice?

1. Let each religion speak for itself. A friend of mine living in India had an interesting conversation with a Hindu about Islam. In all sincerity, the Hindu said, "As you know, Hindus do not eat beef because we worship cows. Similarly, Muslims do not eat pork because they worship pigs." He did not realize how false, even offensive, his assertion was: Muslims do not "worship" pigs; they consider them unclean. But the Hindu man was using his own beliefs to try to interpret what he saw in Islam. Had he understood his error, he would have been horrified. He was not malicious, just ill-informed.

When we assume we understand the worldview of others better than they understand it, we get into all kinds of trouble. The same problem can occur when some Muslims try to explain the Trinity. Across the globe, Christians are accused of worshipping three gods—God the Father, God the Mother, and God the Son. The idea that God would have a physical relationship with a woman and produce a child is as offensive to Christians as it is to Muslims. But instead of going to the source and asking Christians what they believe, some Muslims are content to get their information from non-Christians.

To find out what is important to Muslims, do not watch biased news reports—from liberal or conservative media. Evangelicals should know better. A few years ago, I addressed this tendency in *USA Today*:

> Watching the evening news, you might conclude that evangelicals are hate-filled bigots constantly making vitriolic statements and saying crazy things about hurricanes being caused by immorality. Why? Because, evangelicals are often depicted in news reports as angry people who say crazy things. . . .
>
> As an evangelical leader and researcher, I have no vested interest in—and receive no personal benefit from—speaking out for my Muslim neighbors and friends. Yet, while it is irresponsible not to see the link between radical Islam and terrorism, it is the height of ignorance to assume that all (or most, or even many) Muslims are terrorists.
>
> Don't be so lazy to assume that the worst of a group represents the entire group. They hardly ever do. Perhaps a better idea is to meet them, learn about them and treat them as your neighbor.[8]

---

[8] Ed Stetzer, "Loving All Our Neighbors, Even Our Muslim Ones," *USA Today*, April 26, 2013, https://www.usatoday.com/story/opinion/2013/04/26/islam-boston-terrorism-column/2107447/.

Thus, as Christians, we do the obvious thing: talk to our Muslim neighbors. Doing this allows us to learn what people actually believe. We should not be afraid of this. If we believe, as I do, that we have found the truth—or in my case, that the Truth has found me—then a mutual search for truth will lead people in the right direction.

2. *Talk with and about* individuals, *not generic "faiths."* My second proposal is an extension of the first. We need to develop the habit of talking with and about individuals, not faiths. Many factors influence what a person believes. To know what someone believes based on a single-word label is impossible. No correct sentence can start with the words, "All Muslims in the world agree that ________________," or "Every Christian knows that ________________."

Not long ago, political commentator and television personality Bill O'Reilly appeared on the daytime talk show *The View*. He created an uproar by saying that Muslims were responsible for the September 11, 2001, attacks on the World Trade Center's twin towers in New York City. Two of the hosts left in protest.

According to a *USA Today* report, Feisal Rauf, developer of the proposed Islamic Cultural Center near Ground Zero, said in response to the talk-show incident, "If future generations are to live in a safe and peaceful world, we must break the cycle of misunderstanding and mistrust that encourages extremism here and around the world. Mr. O'Reilly's uninformed comments were offensive, not only to his interviewers, but also to millions of American Muslims."[9]

"Muslims" did not attack the World Trade Center. A handful of Islamist extremists associated with al-Qaeda did. O'Reilly acknowledged this and later backtracked in order to clarify that he did not believe all Muslims were terrorists or responsible for 9/11.

---

[9] Ann Oldenburg, "Imam Rauf: Bill O'Reilly's 'Uninformed' Comments 'Were Offensive,'" *USA Today*, October 15, 2010, http://content.usatoday.com/communities/entertainment/post/2010/10/imam-rauf-bill-oreillys-uninformed-comments-were-offensive/1#.WKLehBJ96Ho.

Similarly, in response to the actions of an American who desecrated a Quran, violent mobs in South Asia attacked Christians and burned their churches and schools. This happened in spite of the fact that a significant number of Christian leaders worldwide publicly decried the desecration. Meanwhile, many Hindus are appalled by the actions of a small minority who use terrorism to advance a political agenda in the name of Hinduism. So, to color an entire religion by the actions of a handful of extremists is unhelpful. Individual believers are not personally responsible for the actions of others who claim affiliation with their group.

3. *Respect others who hold to different beliefs, just as you would expect to be respected for yours.* How can we respect others with different beliefs without compromising our own? Well, we ask them to do the same toward us, even though what we believe sounds rather strange at times—that the true King of the world was born in the backwaters of the Roman Empire, lived a sinless life, died and rose again, and is coming back on a white horse one day. Yet, we would expect a respectful hearing of those beliefs.

Of course, respecting someone and understanding his or her values and beliefs does not mean accepting those beliefs. It is part and parcel of living in a free society to believe that others are wrong. But it is unacceptable to smear leaders, burn books that others consider holy, or equate the radical fringe of a religion with the religion's core beliefs. We must not compare the worst of someone else's religion with the best of our own. Al-Qaeda does not represent mainstream Islam any more than one Quran-burning pastor or the Ku Klux Klan represents Jesus's followers.

I often want to apologize for the excesses of Christian leaders who have misrepresented the Islamic faith and thus strayed from the message of Jesus. When Christians caricature or misrepresent others, we are guilty of violating a teaching of Jesus in the Gospel of Matthew: "Whatever you want others to do for you, do also the same for them—this is the Law and the Prophets" (7:12). As Christians, we have felt the sting of being blamed for actions taken by a radical fringe of our faith—take the Crusades, for instance. It is simply unfair and unchristian to sit by and allow or actively take part in lying about those of another religion.

Part of respecting others with different beliefs is allowing them to proselytize without getting offended. While Hinduism has not traditionally been considered a missionary religion, many modern Hindus have been influenced by the three great missionary religions (Buddhism, Christianity, and Islam). Sects such as the Hare Krishna and Osho are bringing their versions of Hinduism to all corners of the globe.

According to religious scholar Richard Foltz, Buddhism launched "the first large-scale missionary effort in the history of the world's religions" in the third century BC.[10] After his conversion to Buddhism, the Indian emperor Ashoka sent out missionaries to preach the Buddha's message and gather converts throughout South Asia and beyond, eventually touching regions as distant as Greece, Iran, Sri Lanka, and China. Those efforts continue today, and now Buddhists can be found on every inhabited continent.

Seeking converts is a central practice in Islam known as *dawah*, or "invitation." In fact, Yusuf Estes, a former self-identifying Christian who converted to Islam, says that "as Muslims we cannot lie about anything, especially about our religion." Consequently, he says it is impossible to be a Muslim and not invite others to follow "the Straight Path" of Islam. Many Islamic centers in America welcome Christian visitors in order to teach them the basics of Islam and demonstrate that they are not terrorists, and also to seek to convert their neighbors.

Christianity, of course, has been a missionary movement since its beginning. Jesus himself, in his final address to his followers,

---

[10] Richard Foltz, *Religions of the Silk Road: Premodern Patterns of Globalization*, 2nd ed. (n.p.: Springer, 2010), 37.

commanded them to "go, therefore, and make disciples of all nations, baptizing them in the name of the Father and of the Son and of the Holy Spirit, teaching them to observe everything I have commanded you" (Matt 28:19–20). And speaking to Christians everywhere and in all eras, the apostle Paul said, "If I preach the gospel, I have no reason to boast, because I am compelled to preach—and woe to me if I do not preach the gospel!" (1 Cor 9:16 CSB). Sincere followers of any faith would agree: sharing with others the way to right belief is not oppression but in fact an active demonstration of love and concern.

4. We must grant people the freedom to make their own faith decisions. I grew up on Long Island in an Irish Catholic home. Later, God worked in my heart through his Holy Spirit regarding Jesus's death on the cross for my sin, in my place. When I repented of my sin and trusted in Christ by grace through faith, I was given new life in him. I had the religious liberty to respond without restraint.

Earlier I wrote that all religions are not the same. But it does seem to me that most religions have two things in common. First, every major faith teaches its followers, at some point in their sacred texts, not to force others into the faith. Second, some followers in every religion ignore that injunction. The Quran says plainly, "Let there be no compulsion in religion: Truth stands out clear from Error: whoever rejects Taghut [evil] and believes in Allah hath grasped the most trustworthy hand-hold, that never breaks. And Allah heareth and knoweth all things" (QS 2: 256).

In his book *All about Hinduism*, Sri Swami Sivananda, a well-known proponent of yoga and Vedanta, writes, "Hinduism is a religion of freedom. It allows the widest freedom in matters of faith and worship. It allows absolute freedom to the human reason and heart with regard to questions such as the nature of God, soul, creation, form of worship, and goal of life. It does not force anybody to accept particular dogmas or forms of worship."[11]

---

[11] Swami Sivananda, *All About Hinduism* (Himalayas, IND: The Divine Life Trust Society, 2003), 4–5.

Jesus's closest followers had trouble understanding that force was forbidden in religion. One day, on his way to Jerusalem, he entered a Samaritan village. The people of Samaria did not respect the faith of the Jews. Jesus sent two of his closest followers—James and John—to go ahead of him and prepare for them to stay. When the Samaritans refused to receive Jesus, James and John responded angrily, asking if they should call down fire from heaven to punish the people. But Jesus said that the use of force was out of place for his message, and he rebuked both men for making such a suggestion (Luke 9:54–55). Whenever Christians have tried to use force to advance the gospel, they have acted against the wishes of Jesus.

Tragically, while a lack of compulsion is the ideal in each of these religions, it has not always been the reality. In some places in the world, particularly in some radical Islamist societies, compulsion is the norm. Furthermore, I'm aware that some Muslims debate other parts of the Quran regarding compulsion. However, the Muslims in America—the ones that most Christians will encounter—would generally agree with the concerns about compulsion.

So, if this is true globally, then in the spirit of mutual respect and tolerance, Muslims should be free to build a mosque where they live, and Christians should defend their religious freedom to do so.

I am not alone in this line of thinking. In fact, 60 percent of American pastors support Islamic freedom in America.[12] At the same time, Christians should be free to plant churches in places such as Bhutan, the Maldives, Brunei, and Saudi Arabia—where Christian churches are not now.

This book is about engaging Muslims in North America. We must show a better way; that no matter where we live or what religion we follow, we should not demand for ourselves that which we are unwilling to

[12] See my thoughts, despite the title, in Lifeway Research, "Survey: Protestant Pastors View Islam with Suspicion," *Christian Post*, April 23, 2010, http://www.christianpost.com/news/survey-protestant-pastors-view-islam-with-suspicion-44871/.

grant others—freedom from compulsion, freedom from discrimination on the basis of creed, and freedom of conscience. We do so knowing that we must press for such freedom elsewhere while we guard that freedom here. As I explained in a column for Religion News Service, "Religious liberty for some soon means religious liberty for none."[13]

Conclusion

Islam presents many challenges to Christians. As former Obama CIA director Leon Panetta explained, we are in a decades-long war with radical Islam. Naïveté is not a Christian virtue—Islam has a terrorism problem. As CNN's Fareed Zakaria has said:

> There is a cancer of extremism within Islam today. A small minority of Muslims celebrates violence and intolerance and harbors deeply reactionary attitudes toward women and minorities. While some confront these extremists, not enough do so, and the protests are not loud enough. How many mass rallies have been held against the Islamic State (also known as ISIS) in the Arab world today?[14]

However, extremist views do not represent most Muslims—nowhere close. And we can acknowledge both realities: that there are problems, but most of our Muslim neighbors are as concerned with the problems as we are. Thus, we are simultaneously in a multi-faith world with mostly peaceful adherents of world religions at

---

[13] Ed Stetzer, "Burkinis and the Stripping of Religious Liberty," Religion News Service, August 30, 2016, http://religionnews.com/2016/08/30/burkinis-and-the-stripping-of-religious-liberty/.

[14] Fareed Zakaria, "Let's Be Honest, Islam has a Problem Right Now," *Washington Post*, October 9, 2014, https://www.washingtonpost.com/opinions/fareed-zakaria-islam-has-a-problem-right-now-but-heres-why-bill-maher-is-wrong/2014/10/09/b6302a14-4fe6-11e4-aa5e-7153e466a02d_story.html?noredirect=on&utm_term=.62b7450f9063.

our doorstep—including millions of Muslims who are our friends, neighbors, and coworkers. We begin with the humble posture of a learner seeking to understand. Our Muslim neighbors believe differently than we do; but like us, they are people created in the image of God, and they share many of the same struggles we have.

We can, and must, acknowledge the differences and respond as gospel people. Evangelical engagement in North America will be more than this, but it must include sharing our faith with Muslims, just as they are free to share their faith with us. That has always been true—Christianity is, like Islam, a missionary faith at its core.

If we do not share our faith, we will not be faithful to who we are, and we will not love our Muslim neighbors. Without our witness, they will miss out on the truth of *Isa*—"Jesus" in Arabic—the truth that can change their lives as he has changed ours. That is the mission of missions, even when the mission is to Muslims living in North America.

Reflection Questions

1. While reading this chapter, did you learn something new about a religion different from your own?
2. What are the four multi-faith commitments that Christians can make?
3. How might you have been guilty of not letting other religions speak for themselves?
4. How can you connect with a person of a different faith? And how can you engage them on the topic of their faith in an effort to learn more?
5. In the next month, what is one way that you can demonstrate respect to people who believe differently than you do?

2

Overview of Global Islam and Demographics of Islam in North America

Steve A. Johnson

Islam is reportedly the fastest-growing religion in the world, and is predicted to grow significantly in North America over the next decade. In the face of this growth, the Christian church must embrace its call to engage Islam in a missionary encounter with the gospel of Jesus Christ.

For more than 1,400 years, the religion of Islam has been expanding around the world, gaining millions of followers. Historically, Islam has spread by the sword, proselytization, spiritual example, and even financial incentive.

Muslims are united around one core belief: there is one transcendent, immanent God of pure singularity. They further affirm that the Quran is the literal word of Allah, eternally coexisting with him and transmitted to all the prophets beginning with Adam, and yet only purely and completely to Muhammad.

Ed Stetzer encouraged us in the previous chapter to actually talk to individuals from different religious backgrounds. As we consider the Christian church's missionary call to reach all peoples, the contributors to this book have a goal not simply to help you know more about Islam in North America but to help you actually engage with Muslims. This chapter provides an overview of Islam's current growth around the world and in North America, and helps you understand the factors contributing to its growth today. The chapter will also cover the different expressions of the Islamic faith throughout the world, especially in North America. I pray that, with increased awareness of these trends, you will develop empathy for this religious group, particularly those who have left their homeland and moved to North America. I also pray that you will become more at ease with relating to Muslims when you meet them in your communities. As you read this book, I would ask you to pray that the Lord will develop in you a desire to engage your Muslim neighbor with the gospel.

Overview of Projected Growth in Global Islam

According to a 2015 estimate, there are 1.8 billion Muslims in the world, making up a little more than 23 percent of the global population. Islam currently is the world's second-largest religion after Christianity.[1] It is predicted that Islam will continue to grow, and by 2030, it is projected that Muslims will be more than 26 percent of the world's population.[2]

[1] Michael Lipka, "Muslims and Islam: Key Findings in the U.S. and Around the World," Pew Research Center, July 22, 2016, http://www.pewresearch.org/fact-tank/2016/07/22/muslims-and-islam-key-findings-in-the-u-s-and-around-the-world/; Brian J. Grim and Mehtab S. Karim, "The Future of the Global Muslim Population: Projections for 2010–2030," Pew Research Center, January 27, 2011, http://www.pewforum.org/files/2011/01/FutureGlobalMuslimPopulation-WebPDF-Feb10.pdf.

[2] Grim and Karim, "The Future of the Global Muslim Population."

There are two major factors contributing to the rapid growth rate of Islam. Muslims have a higher fertility rate than other religious groups (3.1 births per Muslim family to 2.3 per family within other religious groups), and Muslims are the youngest religion among all religious groups. As a result, many who practice Islam will reach peak childbearing years in the near future.

While future growth is expected, the rate of growth among Muslims worldwide has slowed in recent decades, from 2.3 percent in 1990–2000 to 2.1 percent in 2000–2010. It is anticipated that between 2020 and 2030, the growth rate will be 1.4 percent.[3] The only region where Islam's growth is expected to accelerate is in North America. The number of Muslims in Canada, for example, is forecasted to grow from 2.8 percent to 6.6 percent in the next twenty years.[4]

While the accelerated growth for Islam is based primarily on Muslim birth rates rather than conversions, a recent study suggests that globally among Muslims, Christians, and Jews, Muslims are the only religious group to experience a net growth of individuals converting to the religion rather than converting out of the religion. Worldwide, it is projected that from 2010 to 2050, 1.3 times as many individuals will convert to Islam as will leave it. (Note, however, that this conversion rate is not reflected in the growth of Islam in the United States.) During the same time, Christianity and Judaism are projected to have more individuals converting out of the faith than converting into the faith. For Judaism, two times as many are

[3] Grim and Karim. The growth rate will decline because the population in Muslim-majority countries will be aging. In 1990, more than two-thirds of the Muslim population in those regions were under thirty years of age; by 2010, those under thirty-five years of age comprised 60 percent of the population. This age group is expected to make up 50 percent of the population in those regions. The rate of growth of Christianity for the same time periods is 1.2 percent, 1.0 percent, and 0.6 percent.

[4] Grim and Karim.

expected to convert out, and for Christianity, 2.6 times as many will likely convert out.[5]

Major Islamic Groups Worldwide

In general, Islam focuses on orthopraxy over orthodoxy. Islamic religious practice emphasizes legal interpretations of the major sources of authority within the religion; namely, the Quran and the hadith (a report or account of the words, actions, and habits of Muhammad the prophet). The two major theological schools of thought, or divisions, among Muslims worldwide are the Sunni, constituting 87–90 percent of all Muslims, and the Shi'a, comprising 10–13 percent. Sufis, a brand of Muslims that may be found among both Sunni and Shi'a, are mystical-ascetic groups who focus on the purification of the inner self and the direct experience of Allah.[6]

Islamism is another expression of Islam. It emphasizes the synthesis of more literalist interpretations of the Quran and hadith, along with political involvement with or against Muslim and non-Muslim governments. Two famous Islamist groups within this branch are the Ikhwān al-Muslimūn (Muslim Brotherhood), founded by Ḥasan al-Bannā in March 1928 in Egypt, and the Jama'at-i Islami founded by Sayyid Abul A'la Maududi in August 1941 in India/Pakistan. Both organizations have spread to countries throughout the world, including the United States. Both are also interested in reestablishing the caliphate, which is when a country is under the leadership of a successor to the prophet Muhammad. The last caliphate fell in 1924 with the Ottoman Empire. John Esposito suggested in an online course that one of the main differences between these two

[5] Pew Research Center "The Future of World Religions: Population Growth Projections, 2010–2050," PewForum.org, April 2, 2015, http://www.pewforum.org/2015/04/02/religious-projections-2010-2050/.

[6] J. Spencer Trimingham, *The Sufi Orders in Islam* (New York and Oxford: Oxford University Press, 1998), 1.

Islamist organizations is that the Ikhwān al-Muslimūn tend to rely on grassroots efforts—namely, from the people upward to the political and intellectual elite—whereas the Jamaʿat-i Islami tend to work from the top down.[7]

Salafism is still another expression of Islam, and it takes a very literal approach to interpreting the Quran and hadith, often condemning Sufism and other, more moderate forms of Islam. Salafists reject religious innovation and support the establishment of sharia, Islamic law. Some writers divide Salafists into three categories: the largest group being the purists, who avoid politics; the second-largest group being the activists, who engage in politics; and the smallest group being the jihadists. Most of the violent expressions of Islam come from the jihadist Salafists, which includes groups such as al-Qaeda.[8]

A growing number of Muslims, if not the largest group of Muslims, are only loosely affiliated with one of the classic Islamic groups. Thus, a Muslim might identify as Sunni but not subscribe to a Sunni legal school. This is especially true among Muslims living in the West.

Although they view the Quran and hadith as key sources of authority, progressive Muslims located primarily in the West often take more historical and cultural views of the development of the faith. They now tend to focus on gender inequality, freedom of speech, universal human rights, critical analysis and interpretation of Islamic sources of authority, LGBTQ+ inclusion, separation of religious and state authorities, and repudiating violence.[9]

Recent surveys show that most Muslims in Muslim-populated countries have an unfavorable view of ISIS. For example, nearly

---

[7] John Esposito, Great World Religions: Islam (lecture series), available on the Great Courses website, https://www.thegreatcourses.com/courses/great-world-religions-islam.html.

[8] Marc Sageman, *Understanding Terror Networks* (Philadelphia: University of Pennsylvania Press, 2011).

[9] "MPV Principles," Muslims for Progressive Values website, accessed December 30, 2016, http://www.mpvusa.org/mpv-principles/.

all respondents in Lebanon, and 94 percent in Jordan, disapprove of ISIS; only 14 percent of respondents in Nigeria have a favorable view. Muslims also generally believe that suicide bombings and other forms of violence against civilians in the name of Islam are rarely or never justified, with 92 percent in Indonesia and 91 percent in Iraq holding this view. In a few countries, at least 25 percent of Muslims say these acts of violence are sometimes justified: Palestine (40 percent), Afghanistan (29 percent), Egypt (29 percent), and Bangladesh (26 percent), but again, most Muslims disagree with such violence.[10] In the United States, 48 percent of Muslims say their religious leaders have not done enough to speak out against Islamic extremists.[11]

Muslims in predominantly Muslim countries and non-Muslims in the United States, Russia, and western Europe perceive each other in divergent ways. The top six traits attributed to Westerners by Muslims in predominantly Muslim countries are: selfish, violent, greedy, immoral, arrogant, and fanatical. However, the top five traits attributed to Muslims by non-Muslims in the United States, Russia, and western Europe are: fanatical, honest, violent, generous, arrogant, and selfish. Interestingly, among these two groups, there is unanimity in three traits attributed to the other: violent, fanatical, and arrogant.[12]

Global Muslim Attitudes toward Americans and the United States

In the United States, there has been a steady increase in hate crimes directed against Muslims.[13] There are also an increasing number of

[10] Lipka, "Muslims and Islam."

[11] Lipka.

[12] Lipka. See the chart titled "Characteristics Associated with Westerners and Muslims."

[13] Eric Lichtblau, "Hate Crimes Against American Muslims Most Since Post-9/11 Era," *New York Times*, September 17, 2016, http://www.nytimes.com/2016/09/18/us/politics/hate-crimes-american-muslims-rise.html.

Americans who justify these crimes on the grounds that Muslims reportedly hate America for its values.[14] However, many Muslims love America and American values but also believe that US foreign policy does not reflect those values. To highlight the discrepancy between American values and US government actions, these Muslims point to events and decisions such as the following:

1. The CIA overthrow of the legitimate leader of Iran in the 1950s and its replacement of him with the Shah.
2. The US government's seemingly unconditional support for Israel and its perceived lack of concern for the number of Palestinians being held in refugee camps.
3. The overthrow of Iraq, which killed 2 million civilians and is believed by many Muslims to have destabilized the region, giving rise to ISIS.
4. The overthrow of Libya and the subsequent fragmentation of its culture and institutions.
5. The support for the Saudi regime, whose Wahhabi fundamentalism reportedly gave birth to al-Qaeda and ISIS.[15]

Historical Waves of Muslim Immigration to the United States

While there is evidence that some Muslims were brought to the United States as slaves before 1875, Muslims began to immigrate to the United States in greater numbers beginning at that time, coming mainly from Syria and what are now Lebanon, Jordan, and

[14] Kamran Pasha, "Muslims Don't Hate American Values, but Some Americans Do," *HuffPost: The Blog*, November 22, 2016, http://www.huffingtonpost.com/kamran-pasha/muslims-dont-hate-america_b_13136442.html.

[15] Pasha.

Palestine.[16] They were primarily uneducated and unskilled laborers, but their willingness to work hard rendered them financially successful. And although they had immigrated to the United States in hopes of one day returning to their homeland, most remained in America. This first wave of Muslim immigration lasted until the start of World War I.

The second wave peaked in the 1930s, but it too was ended by war, namely, World War II. For much of this period of mass migration, immigration laws were discriminatory. Thus many immigrants arriving at Ellis Island were turned back, and those from the Middle East experienced difficulty obtaining citizenship. It is reported that at one point they were denied citizenship due to their skin color and even the shape of their noses.[17]

The third wave of immigration took place between 1947 and the mid-1960s as Muslims sought to escape political oppression. Unlike the two previous waves of immigration, Muslims in the third wave tended to be well-educated individuals from influential families. The largest immigrant group was Palestinian, but many also came from Egypt, Syria, Yugoslavia, Albania, and the Soviet Union.

The fourth wave came as the result of the liberalization of immigration laws under President Lyndon Johnson. This wave began in 1967 and, in many ways, continues today. It has been composed primarily of Muslims who are educated, fluent in English, and open to Westernization. Most have been successful in adapting their religious practices to the American culture. The Muslims who wanted to remain in the United States have developed various Islamic

---

[16] Thomas A. Tweed, "Islam in America: From African Slaves to Malcolm X," National Humanities Center website, accessed October 20, 2017, http://nationalhumanitiescenter.org/tserve/twenty/tkeyinfo/islam.htm. See also Peter Manseau, "The Muslims of Early America," *New York Times*, Febrauary 9, 2015.

[17] Syed Dr. Yvonne Y. Haddad, "A Century of Islam in America," *Hamdard Islamicus* 21, no. 4 (1997): 1–7, http://muslimcanada.org/century.pdf.

institutions, including mosques, ethnic clubs, and organizations, such as the Muslim Student Association (MSA).[18]

Various expressions of African-American Islam also began to develop around the start of World War I with the Moorish Science Temple of America movement, which tended to localize in the North and the East Coast states. Its followers established their first temple in 1913 in Newark, New Jersey.

In 1929, upon the death of Timothy Drew, who founded the Moorish Science Temple of America movement, a man with various names—W. D. Fard, Ali Fard, Wallace Fard, and W. F. Muhammad—formed a movement called the Lost-Found Nation of Islam in the West. Eventually, Elijah Muhammad became its leader. The syncretistic form of Islam he created deviated significantly from orthodox expressions of Islam. The group was eventually renamed the Nation of Islam.

Elijah died in 1975, and leadership was assumed by his son, Wallace (Warith) Deen Muhammad, who shifted the movement toward orthodox Islam. It subsequently underwent various name changes, including the American Bilalian Community, but in 1980, the movement became known as the American Muslim Mission. However, some members did not appreciate the changes under Wallace, including one particularly charismatic man, minister Louis Farrakhan. He resigned from Warith's organization and reinstituted the original organization as founded by Elijah Muhammad, maintaining the name Nation of Islam.

A large number of converts to African-American Islam came through the US prison system. A smaller group of converts were Caucasians—primarily women who eventually married Muslim men. A significant number of the Caucasian converts had experimented with various religions and ended up being attracted to

[18] Haddad, 3.

Sufism, the mystical expression of Islam. Today, most African-American Muslims are followers of unaffiliated orthodox expressions of Islam.[19]

Muslims in the United States

A 2016 Pew Research Center survey estimated there were 3.3 million Muslims living in the United States in 2015.[20] This means that roughly 1 percent of the US population is Muslim, but it is estimated that by 2050 the percentage will grow to slightly more than 2 percent.[21] By 2040, Muslims are projected to be the second-largest religious group in the United States, and by 2050, the American Muslim population is projected to reach 8.1 million.[22]

Just over half of the growth of the Muslim population from 2010 to 2015 was due to immigration: Muslims at that time comprised 10 percent of all legal immigrants in the United States. The fertility rate of Muslims was the second most significant factor contributing to the growth of that population. More recently, there has been little net change in the US Muslim population due to conversion: about the same number of Muslim Americans who leave Islam become followers of Islam.[23] (One contributing factor to the large apostasy rate among Muslims in the United States may be that American Muslims are more likely to have non-Muslim friends than are Muslims in other countries.[24])

---

[19] Haddad, 4–6.

[20] Mohamed, "A New Estimate of the U.S. Muslim Population" (see chap. 1, n. 4).

[21] The Muslim population in the United States is not distributed equally across the country. For example, New Jersey has two to three times as many Muslims as the national average.

[22] Mohamed, "A New Estimate of the U.S. Muslim Population."

[23] Mohamed.

[24] Lipka, "Muslims and Islam."

As the number of Muslims in the United States has steadily risen, so has the number of mosques. A 2012 study found that between 2000 and 2012, the number of mosques in the United States grew by more than 900 to a total of 2,106. The largest growth occurred in New York and California, which together accounted for 503 mosques.[25] Not included in the study were Muslim centers on university campuses or any groups lacking a permanent space for prayer.[26] A 2008 investigative report on the Muslim Student Association claimed that as of 2008, this umbrella organization was composed of more than 600 chapters located on or near university campuses.[27] However, only 69 percent of US Muslims say religion is very important in their lives. Most Muslims (96 percent) report they believe in Allah. In terms of religious practice, 65 percent report that they pray at least daily, and 47 percent attend prayer weekly. By these measures, US Muslims are as religious as US Christians, but less religious than Muslims outside the United States.[28]

The founders of the major Islamic organizations in the United States are largely either dead or no longer active. Likewise, the influence of the Ikhwān al-Muslimūn, Jama'at-i Islami, other Salafist organizations, and the ultra-orthodox Salafis is seemingly decreasing and giving way to Muslims born and raised in the United States. While a very small minority among the latter have been radicalized, most are fully acculturated and have embraced American values and lifestyles as they work out ways to integrate these values with their Islamic faith. Among the factors contributing to self-identity,

---

[25] Jaweed Kaleem, "Islam in America: Mosques See Dramatic Increase in Just over a Decade, According to Muslim Survey," *HuffPost*, February 29, 2012, http://www.huffingtonpost.com/2012/02/29/mosques-in-united-states-study_n_1307851.html.

[26] Kaleem.

[27] Investigative Project on Terrorism, "Muslim Students Association: The Investigative Project on Terrorism Dossier" investigativeproject.org, January 1, 2008, 1–39, http://www.investigativeproject.org/documents/misc/84.pdf.

[28] Lipka, "Muslims and Islam."

there are some notable trends that may be significant if they persist over time.

1. In the past, the Saudis tended to significantly control the direction of Islam in America by funding the building of mosques in the United States as well as the salaries of the imams in those mosques (usually men who studied in Saudi Arabia at universities that taught fundamentalist interpretations of Islam). However, Saudi Arabia is losing its influence as indigenous Muslims are increasingly capable of funding their own mosques in the United States.
2. American Muslim leaders are, more often than not, being educated in the United States and obtaining graduate degrees in Islamic studies from secular American universities. In one instance, imams are trained through a Christian seminary, Hartford Seminary in Hartford, Connecticut.
3. American Muslims are developing new, alternative interpretations of Islamic law based on their knowledge of American culture and the traditional authoritative sources of their faith, such as the Quran and the hadith.
4. Foreign-trained Muslim leaders are increasingly judged by Muslim Americans to be irrelevant and ill-equipped to handle the challenges of life as a Muslim and an American citizen.
5. American Muslims are establishing their own schools of higher education to train Islamic leaders; for example, Zaytuna College in Berkeley, California, which was founded by Hamza Yusuf, a Caucasian convert to Sufi Islam.
6. American Muslim women are embracing more feminist interpretations of Islam, which is changing Islamic worship in important ways. For example, Amina Wudud, an African-American Muslim convert, was the first woman to lead Friday community prayer in the United States. A mosque

exclusively for Muslim women now exists in California, and many mosques in the United States are removing the walls within the mosques that have historically separated men and women during worship.

7. More and more Muslims in America, even conservatives, believe that Islam must adapt to the times and the culture.
8. Muslims in America are quite aware of homegrown terrorists within their own population and view it as the responsibility of mosques, Islamic leaders, and Muslim families to address the threat. More often than not, the FBI and local police forces learn about radicalized Muslims from Muslims themselves. A prominent example is the cooperation between mosques and the police in Los Angeles.[29]
9. Muslims in America are moving away from traditional Sunni and Shi'a schools of jurisprudence to create non-denominational interpretations of Islam.
10. Muslims in America are not just entering the traditional American Muslim professions of medicine, sports, and engineering. They are now working in cinematography, social work, law, politics, law enforcement, and education.
11. Muslims in America are frustrated with the Islamophobia they experience in the United States, whether in blatant forms or as microaggression, such as verbal slurs, prejudicial speech, or the tendency to view Muslims as "the other."

---

[29] See Stevan Weine, Ahmed Younis, and Chloe Polutnik, "Community Policing to Counter Violent Extremism: A Process Evaluation in Los Angeles: Report to the Office of University Programs, Science and Technology Directorate, U.S. Department of Homeland Security," National Consortium for the Study of Terrorism and Responses to Terrorism, July 2017, https://www.start.umd.edu/pubs/START_CSTAB_CommunityPolicingtoCounterViolentExtremism_July2017.pdf.

Muslims and United States Politics

Muslims in America tend to support many progressive policy issues while also embracing conservative values and policies. Roughly 90 percent of American Muslims support progressive positions on health care, school funding, the environment, foreign aid, and gun control. However, the majority of US Muslims also support more conservative values, as witnessed by the following: favoring school vouchers (66 percent), government funding for religious social-service groups (70 percent), making abortion more difficult to obtain (55 percent), the death penalty (61 percent), income-tax cuts (65 percent), forcing US citizens to speak English (52 percent), and even stronger laws to fight terrorism (69 percent).[30] Therefore, the attitudes of American Muslims on social issues more closely resemble those of Roman Catholics than of conservative Protestants.

In terms of political endorsement, there has been a considerable shift among American Muslims toward the Democratic Party and away from the Republican Party since 9/11. According to polls conducted over the first decade of the millennium, 23 percent identified as Republican in 2001, but by 2004, only 12 percent identified with the Republican Party. By 2011, only 11 percent identified as Republican.[31]

Conclusion

Islam globally and in the United States is changing rapidly. There are multiple expressions of the faith, such that Muslims are now every bit as diverse as Christians. This makes it difficult, if not impossible, to find a single essence of Islam, a single set of beliefs

---

[30] John Zogby, "American Muslims Have Mainstream Values," *Forbes*, August 26, 2010, http://www.forbes.com/2010/08/26/muslims-polls-mosque-opinions-columnists-john-zogby.html.

[31] Lipka, "Muslims and Islam."

and practices agreed upon by Muslims around the world or even within the United States. Muslim identity is in flux, which means that Christians, if they want to have significant, meaningful relationships with Muslims, must become informed about the shifting landscape of Islam globally and within the United States, and then focus on the uniqueness of the individual Muslim with whom they are interacting.

Reflection Questions

1. How can you overcome the stereotypes Muslims might have of you as a Westerner, and vice versa?
2. How can you overcome your uneasiness, or perhaps fear, of the projected growth of Islam?
3. Muslims and Christians often believe the same things about abortion, modesty, and sexuality. How can you use these commonalities to build bridges with the Muslims in your community?
4. What are some good questions you can ask a new Muslim friend to explore what he or she actually believes?

PART 2

QUESTIONS PEOPLE ASK

3

What Do Christians and Muslims Have in Common?

C. Fyne Nsofor

Christianity and Islam are two separate religions. Moving forward together requires us to be honest about the fact that significant *theological* differences exist between them.[1] At the heart of Christianity is God's self-donating love revealed uniquely in the person and work of Jesus Christ through the Holy Spirit. Christianity affirms the deity of Christ, the inherent moral depravity of man due to the sin of our first parents, and the atoning death of Christ on the cross. Islam, on the other hand, believes that the Christian doctrine of the Trinity is blasphemous and denies the deity of Christ as well as his crucifixion and atonement. Christianity stands or falls on these weighty affirmations and cannot be required to give them up in forging dialogue and understanding. However, both faiths provide us with the mandate and resources for dialogue, understanding, and harmonious coexistence between Christians and Muslims.

[1] See Norman Geisler and Abdul Saleeb, *Answering Islam: the Crescent in the Light of the Cross* (Grand Rapids: Baker, 2002), 233.

On October 13, 2007, 138 Muslim clerics, intellectuals, and leaders signed a document titled "A Common Word between Us and You" (ACW).[2] These leaders sought to identify common ground between Islam and Christianity so that the two faiths could have "a common word" around which to dialogue. ACW opens with the call for peace between Islam and Christianity, declaring, "Without peace and justice between these two religious communities, there can be no meaningful peace in the world." The importance of this call is underscored by the recognition that followers of Islam and Christianity make up over one-half of the world's population. The document proposes that the foundation for this peace is a shared ethic—"love of the One God" and "love of the neighbour." These shared moral and spiritual words provide grounds for interfaith dialogue between Christianity and Islam.

The ACW initiative has continued to receive widespread appreciation and support from both the religious and the nonreligious. A Common Word reemphasizes a real need to pursue dialogue between the two faith communities based on what Christians and Muslims have in common.

We, the contributors to this book, agree that such a multi-faith dialogue is needed. In chapter 1, Ed Stetzer calls for, among other things, a commitment to letting each faith speak for itself and also for us as Christians to show respect to those who believe differently than we do. Later, in chapter 9, D. A. Horton will argue that Christians are more likely to share their faith if they personally engage the people they are seeking to reach and grieve over their spiritual condition. The chapter you're reading builds on these two insights.

One of the purposes of this chapter is to help you understand the spiritual condition of Muslims. It focuses on helping you identify places where there is common ground with Muslims, and to rightly

---

[2] The full text of ACW is available at http://www.acommonword.com/. Since 2007, "A Common Word" has expanded to become a global movement with planned events, publications, university-approved courses, and a growing number of signatories and responses.

understand where there is not common ground. Such observations better equip us for engaging in a missionary encounter with Muslims living in our communities.

The Semitic Family of Religions

Christianity and Islam, as well as their older cousin, Judaism, belong to the Semitic family of religions, often referred to as the "three Abrahamic religions." They share common faith expressions with other religions originating out of early Mesopotamian and Nile River Valley civilizations. Each tradition has its own distinct beliefs and practices, but all three express those beliefs and practices in a world isolated from other religious traditions. Thus, some form of sacred scripture, a commitment to monotheism, and worship and rituals are all common to religions of Semitic origins.

Each faith has a collection of writings considered to be sacred and authoritative in matters of faith and conduct—the Hebrew Bible, the New Testament, and the Quran. In general, both Christianity and Islam take for granted the authority and continuity of the Jewish Bible (the Christian Old Testament). Christianity views the New Testament as the realization of the Old. Islam, being the youngest of the three Abrahamic faiths, also recognizes the Christian New Testament—in its "pristine form"—as God's revelation, but views the Quran as the final and most authoritative document. Before becoming a "book" through long and complicated processes involving a great many communities scattered across time, each of the scriptures of the Semitic family of religions began as oral traditions shaped by and mediated in a variety of locations and contexts.

Abrahamic Faiths

We have already noted the Abrahamic reference to Christianity, Islam, and Judaism. Abraham is a central figure in the scriptures of each faith: he is clearly the ancestor of the Israelites in the Jewish Bible, the spiritual ancestor of Christians in the New Testament, and the physical ancestor of Arabs in the Quran. According to the Old Testament, Yahweh's call of and covenant with Abraham was the beginning of the Jewish people, their special relationship with God, and their mandate to be God's instrument of blessing to all the families of the earth (cf. Gen 12:1–3). In Judaism, the covenant relationship that proceeded through Isaac and the patriarchs is fulfilled in the New Testament (cf. Matt 1:1–2; Heb 1:1–3).

Ibrahim (Abraham) is equally central in the Quran. In the Quran—which is roughly the size of the New Testament—Ibrahim is mentioned in approximately 245 *ayahs* (verses) in twenty-five *surahs* (chapters). Surah 14 bears his name. By comparison, Abraham is mentioned about 300 times in the entire Bible.

According to the Quran, God made Abraham "an Imam to the Nations" (QS 2:124), and together with Ismail (the biblical Ishmael), Abraham built the Kaba or "House of God" in Mecca (QS 2:125).[3] As imam, Abraham is the "foremost," the "model" and "leader in faith." His was the true religion, transcending the Jewish and Christian religions (cf. QS 3:95). In fact, Muslims were to refuse the invitation of Jews and Christians to join their religions in preference to the "true" Abrahamic faith (QS 2:135–36).

Because Abraham is both a unifying and dividing figure, the category "Abrahamic faith" is not without problems. In fact, one concern with grouping these three faith traditions together is that it may suggest a stronger point of contact between Islam and Christianity than is really there. While Abraham has a patriarchal role in all three faiths, significant discord exists about his role in the history of salvation. Nevertheless, the shared recognition of Abraham as a "father of faith" makes dialogue possible and meaningful.

[3] Quranic citations are from *The Holy Quran: Text, Translation and Commentary*, trans. Abdulah Yusuf Ali (Elmhurst, NY: Tahrike Tarsile Qur'an, 2001).

Monotheism: Oneness of God

In December 2015, Larycia Hawkins, a professor of political science at Wheaton College, expressed solidarity with her Muslim neighbor for Advent. She posted two pictures of herself wearing hijab, the Muslim women's veil, on social media and added these words: "I stand in religious solidarity with Muslims because they, like me, a Christian, are people of the book . . . And as Pope Francis stated last week, we worship the same God."[4]

With those five words—"we worship the same God"—she reignited a debate over whether Christians and Muslims indeed worship the same God. This theological question lies at the very heart of Christian–Muslim distinctives, and in chapter 5 of this book, Keith Whitfield tackles the question head-on. At its core is the question of divine identity: the nature and meaning of monotheism in Christianity and Islam.

Do Christians and Muslims worship the same God? Or as Timothy George, dean emeritus of Stanford University's Beeson Divinity School, asked in the title of his 2002 book, *Is the Father of Jesus the God of Muhammad?*

Dialogue must proceed from honest, respectful acknowledgment of the theological positions and differences between Islam and Christianity. As religions of Semitic origins (cf. QS 2:28), Christianity and Islam share a belief in monotheism—the idea of life interpreted in terms of a *personal* God, sin, and judgment in the hereafter. The *Shema* (Heb., "listen," Deut 6:4), the *shahada* (Arabic, "bearing witness"), and the Great Commandment (Mark 12:29–30), respectively, represent the cornerstone of Jewish, Islamic, and Christian passions for the oneness of God. In all three religions,

[4] Manya Brachear Pashman and Marwa Eltagouri, "Wheaton College Says View of Islam, Not Hijab, Got Christian Teacher Suspended," *Chicago Tribune*, December 16, 2015, http://www.chicagotribune.com/news/local/breaking/ct-wheaton-college-professor-larycia-hawkins-20151216-story.html.

reality is viewed as a sacred whole created by a personal God, who sustains life and enforces order. God is involved in creation but is distinct from creation, not limited, controlled, or conditioned in any way by it. God is wholly other than and above everything else, and yet he is concerned and aware of what takes place in the world.

There is not a more significant point of difference between Islam and Christianity than in knowing who God is and how he has made himself known to humankind. Christianity and Islam diverge at this critical theological juncture regarding the meaning and implication of the biblical affirmations that "God is One" and "Jesus is Lord." According to Timothy George, the God of the Bible and the God whom Christians worship is the God "who has forever known himself, and who in Jesus Christ has revealed himself to us, as the Father, the Son, and the Holy Spirit."[5]

Our Shared Humanity

In conversations about religions, one elemental fact is often missed: our shared humanity. Christians and Muslims may differ in their understandings about the identity of God, what is knowable about God, and how sinful humanity can be reconciled with a holy God; but both faiths have the common ground of our humanity. Biblical and Quranic understandings about the origin, nature, and final destiny of humankind coincide at various points. The biblical teaching on both humanity's exaltation over the rest of creation and our lowliness in complete dependence on God for life and provision, is also taught in the Quran.

In each text's creation story and echoes of it, humanity is created (lowly) by God the Creator—"dust from the ground" (Gen 2:7) and "from clay" (QS 15:26); raised (made high) by divine infusion of life-giving energy—"breathed the breath of life into his nostrils"

---

[5] Timothy George, *Is the Father of Jesus the God of Muhammad?* (Grand Rapids: Zondervan, 2002), 55.

(Gen 2:7) and "breathed into him of My spirit" (QS 15:29); and endowed with special faculties to accomplish God-appointed roles. According to Yusuf Ali, "The breathing from God's spirit into man [endowed him with] the faculty of Godlike knowledge and will, which if rightly used would give man superiority over other creatures." Life is a sacred gift of God—"He gave you life" (QS 15:28)—to be cherished, nourished and preserved. Human existence and sustenance are contingent on the love, mercy, and benevolence of God, who provides humankind with all that is necessary for the sustenance of life—"every seed-bearing plant . . . and every tree whose fruit contains seed. This will be food for you" (Gen 1:29 CSB), "brought forth therewith fruits for your sustenance" (QS 2:22).

Humanity owes God absolute allegiance and submission (Deut 6:5–9); and our conduct on earth is to be according to the righteous prescriptions of a holy God, to whom we have to give account in the end. The biblical language of "image of God" is missing in the Quran, and the Quranic man is a free (if limited) moral agent (cf. QS 10:99). The twin ideas of divine blessing and human responsibility are present in the biblical and Quranic visions of man. In Gen 1:28, the biblical man is invested with authority, "blessed," and charged with the mandate—the responsibility—of culture, stewardship, and coregency. In the Quran, man, a being made a little higher than angels (cf. QS 2:30–34), is God's vice-regent on earth (QS 2:30).

The Common Human Predicament and the Need for Salvation

Islam and Christianity share a common perspective about the moral nature of the human predicament. For both faiths, the human predicament is primarily defined as sin—willful violation of the nature and righteous demands of a holy God. In both faiths, as noted earlier, man is created and endowed by God with the faculty of and capacity for moral choice. Both faiths agree with the preacher of Ecclesiastes:

"Fear God and keep His commands, because this is for all humanity. For God will bring every act to judgment, including every hidden thing, whether good or evil" (12:13–14). And both faiths agree that man has failed to live up to the righteous commands of God.

Echoes of the biblical story of the fall of Adam and Eve—our first parents through sin (cf. Genesis 3)—are heard in the Quran (cf. QS 2:35–36). In both the Bible and the Quran, sinful man stands in need of God's mercy and forgiveness. The Muslim who sincerely repents and amends his conduct could be assured of forgiveness, at least this side of eternity; in the Quran, God is *Rahman*, "Most Gracious," and *Rahim*, "Most Merciful." The Muslim should not despair of the mercy of God, because God "forgives all sins" and is "Oft-Forgiving, Most Merciful" (cf. QS 39:53).

There is considerable agreement between Islamic and Christian visions of personal sin and the need for forgiveness, but there are also a few key dissents. Islam and Christianity put a great deal of stress on the sovereignty of God and human responsibility. The primary concern of Islam, however, is God's will, not his nature or character. The Christian faith emphasizes that God's will actually reflects God's character. These differences point to distinctions in belief and practice between these two religions. Islam focuses on obedience to God's will, while Christianity focuses on obeying God because one knows and worships him.

Questions about tensions between the justice of God and the mercy of God, while important in Christian theological thought, are less so in Islam. The fall of Adam is acknowledged in Islam, but the doctrine of original sin is denied. Strong emphasis on personal conduct and responsibility for sin requires no abiding effect of Adam's sin on his offspring. Islamic scholar Ali explains, "We are fully responsible for our acts ourselves: we cannot transfer the consequences to someone else. Nor can anyone vicariously atone for our sins."[6] Without a doctrine of original sin, Islam also denies the doctrine of Christ's atoning death on the cross.

---

[6] Ali, *The Holy Quran*.

Multi-Faith Dialogue

The imperative of multi-faith dialogue and understanding between Christians and Muslims has always existed but has become much more acute in our world today. Multi-faith conversation is an acknowledgment of our distinct theological differences. It does not attempt to minimize the fact that Christianity and Islam are not the same faith. However, it acknowledges that the best of our two faiths demands peace and grace toward one another. Such dialogue also compels us to seek out ways that we can live together in harmony with members of other faiths while we each enjoy a robust commitment to the practice of faith, including the proselytization of those of other faiths. Swiss theologian Hans Küng explains, "No peace among nations without peace among the religions; no peace among the religions without dialogue between the religions; no dialogue between the religions without investigation of the foundations of the religions."[7]

Our world is witnessing a revival of sorts. Religious revivals awaken broad interest in religious matters, infuse freshness into new worship and rituals, and deepen commitments in the individual and collective lives of people of faith. These awakenings are also accompanied by resurgences of fundamentalist ideologies and movements that sometimes diverge into religiously motivated violence, threatening the stability of society and the safety of individuals.

There are an estimated 3.3 million Muslims living in the United States today, a number projected to double by 2050.[8] They are fellow visitors and tourists, immigrants and citizens representing the diverse ethnicities and cultures that make up our country. They are neighbors, friends, homemakers, colleagues at work, business and professional men and women, security and intelligence officers,

---

[7] Hans Küng, *Islam: Past, Present, and Future*, trans. John Bowden (Oxford: One World Publication, 2007), xxiii.

[8] Mohamed, "A New Estimate of the U.S. Muslim Population" (see chap. 1, n. 4).

government employees, and students. They are fellow seekers—sinners in need of reconciliation with the God of Abraham. For the majority of us, our primary interactions with Muslims will not be as religious experts seeking to reconcile Islam and Christianity. Our mandate and privilege will be as individuals, like the proverbial beggar showing another beggar where to find bread. To that end, I recommend the following actions as you prepare to share the gospel with your Muslim neighbors:

- Develop acquaintances and build personal relationships with Muslims. It has been said that people do not care how much you know until they know how much you care. This could not be truer than with cultural or religious others in interfaith conversations.
- Share your prayer needs with your Muslim friends, and pray for them as well. Prayer is important to Muslims.
- Be aware of the diversity of Muslims. Muslims come from around the world and represent varying countries, cultures, and sects. Seek understanding, and be respectful of cultural differences.
- Affirm the religious experience of Muslims. Show appropriate deference to sacred books (the Bible and the Quran) and religious symbols. It will not build better relationships to criticize Muhammad.
- Be prudent with disputed issues and objections. Ask questions rather than assume answers. Remember that individuals may believe something different from official doctrine. Be prepared to lose an argument but win a friend.
- Present the gospel, always keeping the focus on the individual's sinfulness and need for forgiveness and reconciliation with God. Present Jesus: his love, his example, his sacrifice, and the relationship he has with believers.
- Trust God, and depend on the Holy Spirit.

Reflection Questions

1. Where might you find local Muslims? In what ways could you begin to initiate a relationship with them?
2. Would you be able to pray for your Muslim friends in their presence?
3. What questions could you ask of your Muslim friends to better understand their experience with Islam and their particular set of beliefs?
4. Which opportunities can you take advantage of to share the gospel with your Muslim neighbors? Could you establish a regular time to ask the Holy Spirit to help you build relationships with local Muslims, and to also ask him to provide opportunities to share with them how Christ has changed your life?

4

Should We Defend Freedom of Worship for Other Religions?

Bart Barber

July 2015 was a month of strange juxtaposition for me. At the beginning of the month, I attended a religious-liberty seminar. One morning during the seminar, I ate breakfast near Barronelle Stutzman, the floral shop owner who was sued for refusing to provide wedding flowers for a same-sex wedding because doing so would violate her religious convictions. The lawsuit clearly encroached on her rights to operate her business according to her Christian values, yet increasingly, similar cases are being seen.

Meeting Mrs. Stutzman and others who are in similar situations solidified for me that freedom of religion is indeed an inalienable right. We must defend this right for all faiths. Furthermore, as I listened to these people's stories, it became clear to me that one day I will likely have to defend my religious liberty against the imposition of secular progressives. The reality is, we either defend religious liberty for everyone or concede that religious liberty is not a right for anyone. There is no middle ground.

Later in July, I sat in a high school auditorium in Farmersville, Texas, at a local town meeting at which some of my fellow citizens protested the construction of a Muslim cemetery just outside of town. During the meeting, people shouted over the crowd, "You're not welcome here!" The voices in the back of the room were not secular, East Coast progressives; they were Southerners who self-identified as Christians.

If you had asked me before July 2015 if I ever expected to have to fight for religious liberty, I would have answered, "Yes." But I did not expect to have to oppose my neighbors and fellow confessing Christians in doing so.

Of course, I never assume that all Christians agree with my theology and how it applies to public life, particularly regarding religious liberty. Global Christianity is diverse and has never achieved unanimity on religious liberty. But my opponents were not members of Orthodox, Roman, or magisterial churches (and even many of those churches have come to embrace religious liberty); they were members of what we historically refer to as "free churches," or churches separate from state involvement. In fact, the most prominent leader trying to deny religious liberty to these Muslims was a fellow pastor of a local Southern Baptist church. Others in the room opposing the construction of the cemetery were members of my own congregation, and they became angry with me over this issue. The irony in all of this is that Baptists have led the Christian church in articulating and defending religious liberty for all people.

This chapter provides a biblical reflection on the fourth of Ed Stetzer's foundational commitments for Christians living in a multifaith society. He says we need to grant each person the freedom to make his or her faith decisions. That is religious liberty stated in clear terms.

What Is Religious Liberty?

Religious liberty is the freedom to join or leave a religious movement without changing one's relationship, positively or negatively, with the state. At the core of the doctrine is the conviction that the state should not privilege one religion while at the same time denying privileges to another. As individuals, we extend religious liberty to others when we do not seek unique religious privileges from the government for our faith, or petition the government to limit the religious privileges of another faith. In a significant sense, religious liberty cannot be enjoyed by anyone unless it is extended to everyone.

The Christian who proposes to limit Muslims from practicing Islam in the United States undermines principles needed to defend his or her own rights to practice Christianity in the United States. By definition, religious liberty is either for all people or it is for no one.

Changing Times and the Threat to Religious Liberty

I suggest that the events that unfolded in Farmersville, Texas, reflect changing opinions among Christians in America. In part, this change has taken place in response to increased Islamic terrorism and Muslim migration to North America. The 2016 presidential election featured passionate debate about whether First Amendment protections should extend to Muslims, and this debate explicitly arose from concerns about terrorism. Within my own denomination, two separate motions from the floor of the 2016 annual meeting of the Southern Baptist Convention called for the convention to curtail its advocacy for religious liberty whenever such advocacy would benefit Muslims. Both motions failed, but a vocal and surprisingly influential minority of Southern Baptists opposed extending religious liberty to Muslims while seeking to enjoy it for themselves.

Although some Christians do contend for their religious liberty while denying it to others, we must remember that Christ commanded his followers to expect personal persecution and to respect the religious liberty of other people. A starker contrast is difficult to imagine. Failing to extend religious liberty to others is morally wrong and biblically indefensible.

Roger Williams was an early American Baptist pastor who founded the first Baptist church in America. He was also one of the earliest and most ardent supporters of religious liberty in America. Since the end of Williams's ministry (ca. 1603–1683), Baptists have increasingly followed his lead and argued for religious liberty. However, they've typically made their case for religious liberty on philosophical and political terms rather than biblical-exegetical terms. Thus, our biblical conscience for this doctrine has been underdeveloped.

We have come to a point in history at which Christian leaders must rearticulate the case for religious liberty in the words of Jesus Christ rather than the words of British and American political thinkers such as John Locke and Thomas Jefferson.

Biblical Support for Religious Liberty

The Bible contains numerous teachings that highlight this one truth: Christians ought to freely extend religious liberty to those around them. In this section, we'll look at the teaching of the Gospels and listen to Jesus himself speak clearly on this matter. The apostles Paul and John address this subject, and portions of the Old Testament do as well.

As will be shown, religious liberty is a theme that runs throughout the full scope of biblical revelation. When the Bible speaks about religious liberty, it speaks with one voice. The entire canon bears witness to the fact that God's people are called to wait on the Lord, trusting that he rules over the world and will judge the world—all in his perfect timing. Scripturally speaking, the defense of religious freedom ought to be a Christian priority.

A key biblical basis for the doctrine of religious liberty is Jesus's parable of the wheat and the weeds (Matt 13:24–30, 36–43). The parable commands the Christian church to leave alone "the children of the evil one" and to wait patiently for God to bring judgment (v. 38 CSB). Jesus clearly explained that the parable teaches God's intention for his people to grow in their faith and fruitfulness, and for his people to work alongside "the sons of the evil one" (v. 38). This parable serves as a point of correction for Christians. Their first instinct is to take adverse action against the weeds—people outside of the faith—in order to purify the world, but God forbids that they disturb the weeds at all. His reason? God has reserved that job for a specialized squad of angels at the end of the age.

Christ's case for religious liberty is quite different from the arguments offered by unbelievers to support freedom of religion. The Christian case is decidedly different from libertarian, multicultural, or anarchistic arguments for religious liberty. The Christian position affirms that the difference between the wheat and the weeds is of ultimate importance: the weeds should not be in the field; and an ultimate harvest of wheat alone, even if it requires the destruction of the weeds, is just and best.

Where other approaches to religious liberty treat it as a defense of human rights, Jesus's case for universal religious liberty is not primarily based on this. He grounded religious liberty in his respect for the rights of God, not the rights of men. God has selected angels, not human governments, as his agents in the purification of the field because only these angels are qualified to represent his interests in the harvest.

If evangelical Christians believe their own doctrine and know their own history, they will share their heavenly Father's lack of confidence about human ability to conduct the harvest. Evangelical Christians are, by definition, conversionists[1]—they believe that no one is born a Christian, but that all who become Christians enter

[1] Historian David Bebbington has created a definition of evangelicalism now commonly known as "the Bebbington quadrilateral." By this formula, evangelical Christianity lies at the junction of biblicism, crucicentrism, conversionism, and activism. See David Bebbington, *Evangelicalism in Modern Britain: A History from the 1730s to the 1980s* (Boston: Unwin Hyman, 1989).

the faith by being personally born again. Consequently, evangelical doctrine teaches that every Christian at some time in the past was a weed rather than wheat. When Christians deny religious liberty to Muslims and call for the state to impose civil penalties on Muslims indiscriminately, God's people are inadvertently inflicting damage on possible future wheat that they simply are not yet able to identify.

Historically speaking, when Christian believers have supported suspensions of religious liberty in order to repress Islam, they have harmed themselves in the process, bringing oppression on themselves. One example of this type of outcome is found in the First Crusade. Christians originally inaugurated the Crusades as a war against Muslims. Yet by 1209, Pope Innocent III had proclaimed a crusade against a Christian sect (the Cathars), resulting in genocide in southern France. At the battle of Béziers on July 21, 1209, Catholic crusaders massacred the entire population of the city, Catholic and Cathar alike, under the benediction and absolution of the pope.

Humans do not skillfully wield the sickle with anything approaching precision. With good reason, God the Father, in the interest of protecting the wheat, forbids his people to eliminate the weeds by their own devices.

Jesus said something more terse but strikingly similar when he told his disciples to "leave [the Pharisees] alone" to meet their own fates, since they "will be uprooted" anyway (Matt 15:12–14). Just two chapters after the parable of the wheat and the weeds (13:25–40), Jesus made a brief reference to the parable to urge his disciples not to fret over offending those who reject Jesus's message or to take action against those who take offense (15:13).

From this passage we learn that the parable of the wheat and the weeds was not simply a onetime lesson that Jesus taught (although one time would be enough to direct our thinking on religious liberty). This reference represents a memorable theme to which Jesus returned when he needed to remind his disciples how to deal with their spiritual opponents. The apostles included these episodes in the Scriptures because they knew that their disciples also needed to know the Christian way to interact with people who rejected the gospel and rejected believers. This need endures into the twenty-first century.

Jesus rebuked his disciples when they wanted to punish a Samaritan village for rejecting him (Luke 9:51–56). He explained that his otherworldly kingdom employs testimony, not force, to accomplish its mission (John 18:36–37). And even when those who hold other faiths persecute Christ's followers, he commanded them to choose the way of prayer, not of retaliation (Matt 5:43–48). These instances are noteworthy. So is his absolute omission of any teachings urging his followers to strike out against people for unbelief or to appeal for governmental action that would disfavor those who affirm another religion. The "red-letter" case for granting religious liberty to all, including Muslims, is incontrovertible.

Of course, all Scripture, not just Jesus's statements, is inspired by God and is beneficial. And the exegetical case for religious liberty extends beyond the Gospels. Early defenses of religious liberty also considered the apostle Paul's teachings about the nature of government in Romans 12–13. A fairly robust theology of religious liberty could arise out of Rom 12:18 alone: "If possible, as far as it depends on you, live at peace with everyone" (AMP). If Scripture commanded believers to live at peace with any willing Roman or Judean—citizens of the first states ever to shed the blood of Christian martyrs—how can this command not apply to each and every Muslim willing to live at peace with her or his neighbors?

Paul's stern rebuke of the Corinthian church in 1 Corinthians 5 is highly relevant. He wrote, "What business is it of mine to judge outsiders? Don't you judge those who are inside? But God judges outsiders. Put away the evil person from among yourselves" (vv. 12–13). This apostolic scolding upbraids any church that is ready to take punitive action against non-Christian outsiders while taking no action against unrepentant sin within the church's membership.

When we take it upon ourselves to punish outsiders for their unbelief, we attempt to wrest authority from God that he has not given us. That we do so while leaving tasks undone that he actually *has* assigned to us is an affront to Christ's lordship over the church.

In his second letter to the church at Corinth, Paul was primarily addressing the discipline of believers. Still, he made a general statement about how believers ought to wage war against spiritual error, against "every high-minded thing that is raised up against the knowledge of God" (2 Cor 10:3–5). This is a category that certainly includes Islam and other non-Christian theologies. To support religious liberty for all is not to raise the white flag of surrender in the spiritual war that engulfs us. Rather, it is to set aside the peashooters of physical force and take up the advanced weaponry of the spiritual realm.

In John's Apocalypse, when the martyrs for the faith cry out that their blood might be avenged, they receive an answer that lines up perfectly with the parable of the wheat and the weeds: they are commanded to wait patiently for God to bring forth his judgment at his appointed time (Rev 6:9–11). The New Testament response to even the most hostile opponents of the Christian faith is a consistent reliance on spiritual strategies, not earthly ones—a willingness to wait for the throne of heaven to take action, rather than urging human government to preempt the Lord's hand.

What about the Old Testament? Proponents of religious liberty have not ignored the first part of the canon. In *The Bloudy Tenent,* Roger Williams cited fifty of the sixty-six books in the Protestant canon, using multiple passages from all of those (except 2 Kings and Jude).[2] The Christian doctrine of religious liberty, like most ortho-

---

[2] Roger Williams, *The Bloudy Tenent of Persecution for Cause of Conscience Discussed; and Mr. Cotton's Letter Examined and Answered* (London: J. Haddon, 1848). The full text of this book has been posted by Archive.org at https://archive.org/stream/thebloudytenento00willuoft/thebloudytenento00willuoft_djvu.txt.

dox Christian doctrines, requires that the Christian employ the New Testament as the interpretive key for the Old.

Ancient Israel was a theocracy. No one disputes that. Was that Old Testament political experiment a success to be emulated or a failure to be avoided? Jesus's own evaluation of Old Testament Israel is pertinent. Although Israel was consistently ineffective at suppressing idolatry, Jesus noted that the Jewish theocracy was tragically effective at "[killing] the prophets and [stoning] those who [were] sent to [it]" (Luke 13:34). The seventeenth-century advocates for religious liberty turned frequently to precisely those stories—the travails of both Daniel (who suffered under a pagan government) and Jeremiah (who suffered under a Jewish government)—as evidence that human governments fail, and miserably so, when they try to enforce right belief as they see it.

Christian support of religious liberty is distinctly eschatological in the sense that the doctrine depends on an understanding that Christ's first coming inaugurated something new that awaits full realization at his second coming.[3] History falls into at least three epochs: the time before Christ, the time from his coming until his return, and the time after his return. A passage from Paul's sermon on Mars Hill features these three epochs: "Therefore, having overlooked the times of ignorance, God now commands all people everywhere to repent, because He has set a day when He is going to judge the world in righteousness by the Man He has appointed. He has provided proof of this to everyone by raising Him from the dead" (Acts 17:30–31).

First, the "times of ignorance" extend up until the "now" that God has established after "raising [Christ] from the dead." The Old Testament theocracy existed during the "times of ignorance." Second, Christ now sits on the throne of David as God promised in the past. Finally, the Father has set a day, Paul declared, when eschatological judgment will take place. Who will usurp this throne of David from

---

[3] Curtis Freeman, "Roger Williams, American Democracy, and the Baptists," *Perspectives in Religious Studies* 3 (Fall 2007): 267–86.

Christ that they might begin the judgment of unbelievers before the day the Father has set?

In Paul's sermon at Athens, we see the important connection between religious liberty and evangelism. The sermon is, after all, an evangelistic sermon, and the topic is explicitly God's relationship with false religion. God has ended the "times of ignorance." God has withheld until later the "day when He is going to judge the world." Between these two times, God "commands all people everywhere to repent."

Paul's sermon draws attention to three gifts from God. The first is God's forbearance concerning judgment, which is rightly deserved during the times of ignorance. The second is God's corroboration of the gospel by means of the resurrection of Jesus. The third is God's willingness to hear human repentance. One way of regarding religious liberty is that by it, human governments leave room for human repentance, for repentance is only genuine when it arises out of remorse and not out of coercion.[4]

Responding to Objections

In conclusion, a consideration of some common objections is in order.

Some Christians claim that Islam does not deserve religious liberty because it is not a religion. It is alleged that Islam is a "geo-political movement that has basically set itself against Western

[4] The 2011 document "Christian Witness in a Multi-Religious World: Recommendations for Conduct"—jointly produced by the World Council of Churches, the Pontifical Council for Interreligious Dialogue, and the World Evangelical Alliance—features a recent and bold statement of the principle that true evangelism requires the hearer to be at full liberty to accept or reject the gospel: "If Christians engage in inappropriate methods of exercising mission by resorting to deception and coercive means, they betray the gospel and may cause suffering to others."

Civilization."[5] Also, Islam does not generally extend religious liberty to other faiths; therefore, objectors suggest that Muslims should not enjoy religious liberty. Finally, a great deal of violence takes place worldwide under the auspices of various Islamic sects, and so objectors claim that Christians can only enjoy physical safety if religious liberty is withdrawn from Muslims.[6]

These objections are not valid because Christ's commands to extend religious liberty to others arise out of a context that anticipates each of these objections. Every religion entails a theory of geopolitics, and every state church in the history of Christendom has been as much a geopolitical movement as Islam is today.

Jesus proclaimed religious liberty in the context of a Greco-Roman fusion of state and religion that could serve as the paradigmatic expression of geopolitics masquerading as religion. If Christ required that Christians extend religious liberty to the Roman geopolitical religion, why wouldn't his commands apply equally to Islam? Furthermore, in both Second Temple Judaism and Greco-Roman religion, Christianity encountered established religions that refused to extend religious liberty to Christians, resorting sometimes to violent means in their efforts to extirpate the Way. The Lord, the apostles, and the church fathers met these religious establishments, not with legislation and armaments, but with prayer and the gospel. And they won!

Christians must defend religious liberty for Muslims so that our hands will be clean. Too many sects of Christianity wear the blood of martyrs on their hands. Evangelical Christians should be careful not to lengthen this tragic history.

Christians must defend religious liberty for Muslims rather than shut doors of opportunity to bring Muslims to faith in Christ.

---

[5] Gerald Harris, "Do Muslims Really Qualify for Religious Freedom Benefits?" *Christian Index*, June 6, 2016, https://christianindex.org/muslims-really-qualify-religious-freedom-benefits/.

[6] Harris.

Evangelicals must choose between the way of religious coercion and the religious voluntarism that has defined our understanding of the gospel and the manner of its proclamation.

Christians must defend religious liberty for Muslims so that we will be children of our Father who is in heaven, who causes his sun to rise on the evil and the good, sends rain on the righteous and unrighteous, and gives liberty of conscience to Christian and Muslim alike. Christ has commanded it. The proclamation of the gospel thrives in it. Christian duty demands it.

Reflection Questions

1. What is the definition of religious liberty?
2. In what way is Christian support of religious liberty specifically biblical?
3. How might you contend for religious liberty in your community for those who disagree with you?
4. How would you explain the importance and impact that defending the Muslim's religious liberty has for the Christian?

5

Do Christians and Muslims Worship the Same God?

Keith S. Whitfield

At the beginning of 2017, my family took a trip to a predominantly Muslim country in Southeast Asia. It was the first cross-cultural experience for my eleven-year-old son and soon-to-be thirteen-year-old daughter. We had a great time exploring the culture, meeting new people, and enjoying new foods.

My kids had a lot of questions before the trip about what it would be like to be in another country, if it would be safe to travel outside the United States, whether or not the food would taste good, and so forth. While we were in Asia, they had more questions. They asked about the cultural differences that they experienced. They wondered if they had to eat everything served to them. They asked why people wanted to take photos with them.

After we returned home, the conversations went deeper. One morning, on the way to school, my son and I were talking about our trip. I asked him what he thought about the experience. Like a typical eleven-year-old, at first he said, "I don't know." But then he asked, "Don't we all worship the same God?" I was not expecting that question. I had four minutes and twenty-seven seconds to answer it before I would drop him off at school. I could only give him a short answer. So I said to him that Muslims and Christians don't worship the same God, because Muslims don't believe Jesus is God.

While I believe that the answer I gave my son is the right answer, my short conversation with him was not sufficient to explain why his question is so important to understanding the difference between Islam and Christianity and helping us engage Muslims with the gospel. We as Christians need an in-depth understanding of the doctrine of the Trinity. It is a central doctrine of our faith, and we will be fruitless in our efforts to witness to Muslims, who deny the Trinity, if we ourselves lack an understanding of the doctrine and cannot accurately explain it.

The Timing of the Question

Islam is the fastest-growing religion in the world. Between now and 2050, the population of Muslims in the United States is expected to increase from 1 percent to 2 percent. In Canada during this same period, Muslims are expected to grow to 6.6 percent of the country's population.[1] This demographic change provides missional opportunities for evangelical Christians. Followers of the second-largest religious group in the world will be living in our neighborhoods.

Christians are called to make disciples of all nations by sharing God's love as demonstrated in the sending of his Son to die for the sins of all people. Religious differences, however, can create tension between people of different faiths. In North America, we often struggle with having honest and open conversations about real religious differences. This difficulty becomes more acute when those with different beliefs enter our communities and we experience changes as a result of their presence. The points of tension may tempt us to find superficial common ground and ignore the differences.

[1] Grim and Karim, "The Future of the Global Muslim Population" (see chap. 2, n 2).

One place where we see this desire to diminish differences comes when we ask, "Do we worship the same God?" This is not a new question. In 1076, Gregory VII discussed this issue in a letter to Al-Nasir, king of Mauritania. He claimed that Muslims and Christians worship the same God, but they know him in different ways. In 1965, Vatican II took a position on this issue that reflects what Gregory VII had written. In the United States, the importance of the question was revived after the terrorist attacks in New York and Washington, DC, on September 11, 2001.

The pressure to affirm that Christians and Muslims worship the same God was applied to alleviate the religious, cultural, and political strain between followers of the two religions. As one book suggests, "To ask: 'Do we have a common God?' is, among other things, to worry: 'Can we live together?'"[2] In November 2003, during an interview with ABC news anchor Charles Gibson, George W. Bush provided an answer to the question. He said, "I think we do. We have different routes to get to the Almighty."[3]

According to a recent survey, Americans are evenly divided over whether Christians and Muslims pray to or worship the same God. Forty-six percent of Americans believe that Christians and Muslims do worship the same God. Among North American evangelical Protestants, 35 percent believe this. Interestingly, when asked if Islam is similar to Christianity, only 34 percent of Americans and 26 percent of evangelical Protestants agree that it is.[4] When the question shifts from the identity of the one who is worshipped to the

[2] Miroslav Volf, ed., *Do We Worship the Same God?: Jews, Christians, and Muslims* (Grand Rapids: Eerdmans, 2012), vii.

[3] ABC News, "Bush on Religion and God," ABC News, October 26, 2004, http://abcnews.go.com/Politics/story?id=193746&page=1.

[4] Ed Stetzer, "Christianity and Islam: Evangelicals and Americans Are Not on the Same Page About the 'Same God,'" *Christianity Today*, December 22, 2015, http://www.christianitytoday.com/edstetzer/2015/december/christianity-and-islam-how-do-people-see-them-and-who-they-.html.

nature of the religion and its teachings, people seem to recognize the differences more clearly.

The Difficulty with the Question

After the George W. Bush interview, the *Christian Century* published five articles from scholars with different theological backgrounds to address whether Muslims and Christians worship the same God.[5] Three Christian scholars, a Jewish scholar, and a Muslim scholar illustrated the complexity and importance of the question. Most interesting, none of the contributors answered the question with an unqualified "yes." Everyone answered with a "sort of yes" and "sort of no." Each of them affirmed "same" if one is considering only basic divine attributes. But that affirmation does not say much about "who" God is. Both religions teach that God reveals himself in human history through divine acts and sacred texts, but one cannot affirm that Christians and Muslims worship the same God under these terms.

The desire for unity among people is a noble desire, but we can't affirm unity and ignore the complex and profound differences in what we believe. Yes, Muslims and Christians teach that God reveals himself in history. They agree with one another that God does exist and that he is one. They both affirm that there will be divine judgment at the end of human history. They agree that there is a heaven and a hell.

Beyond these agreements, North American Muslims and Christians share other values. They both have regard for the relative freedom and economic opportunities that living in North America affords them. Also, they value the practice of acknowledging the equality and dignity of all people. Nevertheless, Islam and Christianity are not the same faith.

---

[5] Jon D. Levenson, "Do Christians and Muslims Worship the Same God?" *Christian Century* 121, no. 8 (April 20, 2004): 32–33.

Christians affirm that there is one God, and that Jesus is the eternal, divine Son of God, who is equal with his Father in every way. Muslims affirm that there is only one divine person. Thus, they claim that Christians worship not one God, but three gods. Muslims also teach that Muhammad has a unique authoritative role as the final prophet of Allah. Christianity teaches that Jesus is the last Word from God (Heb 1:2).

According to the Bible, Jesus is the true and final revelation of God. On the basis of this, he sets the path for how to know and come to God. Jesus says, "I am the way, the truth, and the life. No one comes to the Father except through Me" (John 14:6). But in Islam, the Five Pillars (faith in Allah, five daily prayers, giving to the poor, fasting, and pilgrimage to Mecca) provide the exclusive boundaries for Muslim practice and identity. These important distinguishing features of Islam and Christianity cannot simply be overlooked.

A New (and Better) Question

Timothy George suggests that we reframe the conversation.[6] Instead of "Do Christians and Muslims worship the same God?" he proposes a new question: "Is the Father of Jesus the God of Muhammad?" Stating the question in these terms avoids some of the confusion that comes with the "yes" and "no" answers to the first question.

When we address the question, "Is the Father of Jesus the God of Muhammad?" we are not trying to locate the lowest common denominator between Christianity's concept of God and Islam's concept of Allah. We are not constrained to consider the question from our commitment to monotheism but are led to affirm (at some level) that there's only one God to worship. The reframed question helps us address the issue from the reality and identity of the God we know. We are emphasizing that to know God is to know him

[6] George, *Is the Father of Jesus the God of Muhammad?* (see chap. 3, n. 5).

through the way he has revealed himself. The real question is: "Who is worshipping the true God the way he desires to be worshipped?" This question undoubtedly causes tension because it suggests exclusive knowledge of God by one religion over another. But that is why it is a crucial missional question.

Reframing the question focuses our attention more clearly on the centrality of the Fatherhood of God in Christianity and helps us recognize just how foreign fatherhood is to the identity of Allah in Islam. The teachings of Islam and Christianity on the identity of God differ most clearly at this very point. In Christianity, the Fatherhood of God is revealed clearly in the person of Jesus and his relationship with his Father. John wrote in his Gospel that no one has seen the Father except for the Son, and he came to make the Father known (14:9).

The Fatherhood of God is the foundation of the Christian doctrine of the Trinity. It is expressed in the very way that God reveals himself to us first and foremost (see Ps 103:13; Jer 3:19). God the Father establishes his unique, covenantal relationship with Israel as a Father/son relationship. Israel is called "My firstborn son" (Exod 4:22; cf. Deut 1:31). He leads them through the wilderness like a father, and when needed, he disciplines them as a father disciplines a son (Deut 8:5). When Jesus comes to earth in his incarnational ministry, the Father twice heralds from heaven (at Christ's baptism and on the Mount of Transfiguration) that Jesus is "My beloved Son" (Mark 1:11; 9:7; cf. Matt 3:17; 17:5; Luke 3:22; 9:35). At the end of his ministry, Jesus tells his disciples that he will return "to My Father and your Father—to My God and your God" (John 20:17). The writers of the New Testament letters witness to the Fatherhood of God: "the God and Father of our Lord Jesus Christ" (Eph 1:3; 1 Pet 1:3; cf. 2 Cor 11:31).

God reveals himself most fundamentally as Father, not as Creator, Ruler, or the Almighty One.[7] God is eternally Father; he

---

[7] Michael Reeves, *Delighting in the Trinity* (Downers Grove: InterVarsity, 2012), 23.

did not become Father only when he acted in creation. Everything he does, he does as Father. The apostle John's call for the church to love one another is based on the Fatherhood of God. First John 4:7–8 says, "Dear friends, let us love one another, because love is from God, and everyone who loves has been born of God and knows God. The one who does not love does not know God, because God is love." In Christianity, "love" is the way God is toward himself (the Father's love for the Son and the Spirit) and toward his people. If you know him, you love him. You love him because he loved you first (1 John 4:9–10).

The Christian doctrine of the Trinity is criticized in the Quran. Surah 5:72–75 dispels the doctrine, claiming that Christians believe in three gods, and rejects the Fatherhood of God. Surah 112:1–4 says, "He is Allah, the One and Only; Allah, the Eternal, Absolute; He begetteth not, nor is He begotten; And there is none like unto Him." In these statements, it is not clear that the Christian doctrine is rightly understood. Perhaps the confusion results from Christians in the early seventh century who taught heresy about God. Islam emerged just over 150 years after the Chalcedonian council solidified the Christian teaching on the divine and human nature of Jesus and the doctrine of the Trinity. During this time, it appears that some Christians living in or near Mecca still believed incorrect doctrines about the nature of Jesus and about the Trinity. Nevertheless, in the Quran, Jesus is presented to us as merely a messenger (QS 4:171).

Christianity and Islam differ on the doctrine of the incarnation, the Trinity, and the deity of Christ, and the redeeming effect of the cross of Jesus and his resurrection. When Christians say they worship God, they mean that they worship the triune God. The Bible affirms there is one God who exists in three distinct persons: Father, Son, and Holy Spirit. The triune nature of God is central to the distinctive, orthodox beliefs of Christianity.

The early Christian confessions are structured around the trinitarian confession. In the Apostles' Creed, the whole of the Christian faith is summarized around the trinitarian formula. There are three articles in the creed. Each begins with a confession of belief. The first one says, "I believe in God, the Father Almighty." The two subsequent articles confess belief in the Son and in the Spirit. The Athanasian Creed begins by declaring the centrality of the Trinity to the Christian faith and to the knowledge of who God is. It reads, "Whosoever will be saved, before all things it is necessary that he hold the catholic faith; which faith except everyone do keep whole and undefiled, without doubt he shall perish everlastingly. And the catholic faith is this: that we worship one God in Trinity, and Trinity in Unity."

The Christian faith is about knowing God. It is not about merely paying homage to him or merely acknowledging his existence. It is about knowing him as the One who is personal and as the One who created a people for the purpose of dwelling with them. God has revealed himself to us so that we may know him, and more importantly, know him as triune. In the Bible, life is maintained by knowing and worshipping God (Gen 2:15–17; John 17:3; Rom 8:1–3; Eph 4:17–18). We were created for the purpose of knowing our Creator. But when sin entered the world and impacted the human condition, our knowledge of God became distorted. The redeeming work of God restores our knowledge of him and our worship of him.

Because God has revealed himself to us through the incarnation of his Son and through the revelation of his Word, we can know the triune nature of God. In fact, to know God is to know him as being three in one. Some people see the doctrine of the Trinity as a historic confession of the Christian faith but largely irrelevant to the practical realities of Christianity. The truth is, if God were not triune, we would lose essential attributes of his divine nature. This confession communicates the personal, compassionate, and active benevolence of the God of Christian Scripture.

God is triune. The most important Christian confession about the character of God is "God is love." He could not be loving by nature if there were no one to love before creation. He could not be a Father without a child. He is both loving and Father. He did not create to be either loving or a Father. Jesus says in John 17:24, "Father, . . . You loved Me before the world's foundation." God the Father is the Father of Jesus, the eternal Son. God finds his identity, his Fatherhood, in loving and giving out his divine life to the Son (Heb 1:3).

The Christian doctrine of salvation is predicated on the doctrine of the Trinity. Jesus explains the trinitarian nature of salvation in John 17:20–26. Jesus was sent into the world because the world does not know the Father (v. 25; cf. 1:14, 18). He was qualified for this task because he knows the Father and has known him fully from all eternity (v. 25; cf. 1:1–3, 18). Christ declares that the salvation he brings to the world is salvation generated by the love of God the Father (v. 26; cf. 3:16; 1 John 4:8–10), and that salvation produces love in the redeemed (v. 26; cf. John 3:16; 13:34–35; 1 John 4:8–10). The Father sent the Son to make himself known. He did not send Jesus to merely reveal information about him, but that we would know him as loving Father. Jesus says, "I made Your name known to them and will [continue to] make it known, so the love You have loved Me with may be in them and I may be in them" (John 17:26).

Jesus is the eternally loved Son of the Father. He came to share with us the love that he has with his Father. The writers of the New Testament proclaim that when God redeems believers from sin and death, Jesus is our merciful High Priest, who is not ashamed to call us brothers (Heb 2:11), and we are adopted as children into God's family. Christians become children of God the Father too (John 1:12–13). J. I. Packer is right when he says one's understanding of Christianity is reflected in their understanding of the Fatherhood of God:

> If you want to judge how well a person understands Christianity, find out how much he makes of this thought of being God's child, and having God as his Father. If this is

> not the thought that prompts and controls his worship and prayers and his whole outlook on life, it means he does not understand Christianity very well at all.[8]

The shape of Christian salvation depends on the doctrine of the Trinity. The Father sent the Son into the world to make the Father known through his life, death, and resurrection. It is in knowing the Son and the Father that we become united with Christ and receive eternal salvation. The knowledge of the triune God's work of salvation for us is revealed to us by the Spirit, who is one with the Father and the Son. Thus, Christians are baptized in the name of the Father and the Son and the Holy Spirit (Matt 28:19).

What makes Christianity distinct from other religions is the identity of our God as the triune One. The bedrock of our faith is nothing less than God himself, and every aspect of the Christian story—creation, revelation, and salvation—is Christian, and only Christian, if it is understood to be the work of the triune God. We may believe in the death of a man called Jesus, his bodily resurrection, and salvation by grace, but without the doctrine of the Trinity, we are unable to believe that he is God and that his work is the very work of God. The truth is, if we don't affirm the triune God of the Christian faith, we can't affirm the Christian gospel. The Trinity is the governing center of all Christian belief.

How to Talk about the Trinity

Two of Ed Stetzer's foundational principles for living in a multi-faith world instruct us in our missionary encounter with Islam in North America. He encourages us: (1) to engage individuals and not generic "faiths," and (2) to respect the beliefs of people from other religions. There is a tendency to hold one's religious convictions and forget

[8] J. I. Packer, *Knowing God* (Downers Grove, IL: InterVarsity, 1993), 201.

to follow these two principles. We should guard ourselves from this temptation.

Yes, as Christians we deny the infallibility of Muhammad's revelation and reject that Muhammad is the final prophet. But the missionary engagement that we are called to requires us to engage individuals who are convinced that they know the one true God. They hold these beliefs deeply. We have to engage them in a loving way by listening to them, and we engage them by sharing the compelling biblical story of how God the Father has sought to redeem them by the atoning work of his very own Son. In this way, the doctrine of the Trinity distinguishes Christianity from Islam and Judaism.

Christians who attempt to share the gospel with Muslims often struggle with how to explain the Trinity. Muslims are quick to argue against the Trinity. They claim Christians worship three gods, and they dismiss the teaching that God has a son. These difficulties have caused many followers of Christ to avoid bringing up the subject altogether. We have to be able to give a reasonable understanding that does not sound like polytheism.

I have argued in this chapter that you cannot ignore the doctrine of the Trinity because it is central to the Christian faith. So how do you talk to Muslims about this doctrine and explain what Christians actually believe?

Timothy Tennent is right: monotheism provides a bridge for Muslims to understand and receive the Christian gospel. Tennent says:

> I am still prepared to hail the emergence of early Arabian monotheism as a positive development, a potential *preparatio evangelica,* which may yet serve as a bridge for Islamic peoples to cross over and receive the Christian gospel. In short, despite our differences, Christians need not speak disparagingly about Muhammad or Islam. Christians can celebrate with Muslims their timely rejection of idolatry and their acceptance of monotheism. Indeed, these are wonderful examples of God's grace and fulfillment of his promise

> to use Abraham to bless all peoples (Gen. 12:1–3) as well as his promise to make the descendents of Ishmael a great nation (17:20; 21:11–13).[9]

The affirmation that Muhammad is the last prophet of Allah is central to Islam. This core conviction is articulated in the *shahadah*, the foremost confession of Islamic faith: "There is no god, but Allah, and Muhammad is the prophet of Allah." One may say Christianity and Islam share some concepts for articulating their understanding of who God is—resemblances that make Islam and Christianity more similar to one another than to Eastern religions such as Buddhism, Confucianism, Hinduism, and Taoism. Thus, monotheism can be a viable bridge insofar as Christians can rightly handle the question of this chapter by both affirming monotheism and providing a trinitarian accounting of Christian beliefs.

We must acknowledge that the doctrine of Trinity does mean that the Christian view of God is different from Islam's view of Allah. But the Trinity is not what the average Muslim thinks it is. Before trying to explain the doctrine, we should listen to what the person we are talking to actually thinks it means for Christians to view God as triune.

While our discussion of the Fatherhood of God and its relationship to the Trinity is important, it is equally important for us to maintain and demonstrate to a follower of Islam that Christians clearly affirm monotheism. You can show them this truth from the Bible. In Deut 6:4 and Exod 20:3, monotheism, the core theological belief of Islam, is affirmed. This Christian teaching is not limited to the Old Testament. Jesus (Mark 12:28–31) and the apostle Paul (Acts 17:22–31; 1 Cor. 8:4–6) also taught that God is one. Affirming monotheism establishes that Christianity does not teach

---

[9] Timothy C. Tennent, *Theology in the Context of World Christianity* (Grand Rapids: Zondervan, 2007), 44.

that there are three gods. However, it may not help Muslims come to terms with what we mean by "Trinity."

The Trinity is not a mathematical formula. It is not 1 + 1+ 1 = 1. That's incoherent. If we think of the Trinity as a mathematical formula, the followers of Islam would be right that Christianity would believe in three gods. 1 + 1 + 1 = 3. There is only one God, who is all-powerful, all-knowing, present everywhere, completely sovereign, and he alone is worthy of worship. The trinitarian doctrine teaches there is one God, who subsists as three persons (Father, Son, and Holy Spirit).

The glorious truth found in the Christian doctrine of the Trinity is we can truly know God. Christianity and Islam both affirm that God spoke through prophets. When God speaks through prophets, the people don't encounter God himself. They hear a voice that is a reflection of God's voice. We see this happening in the Old Testament. When God spoke to Moses on top of Mount Sinai, the Scriptures reveal, God's voice was like peals of thunder. But when the people of Israel heard the words of God, they heard Moses's voice. It was a true manifestation of God's voice. It reflected how God appeared to be. But from that revelation, we don't know him as he is. This phenomenon is not unique to Judaism or Christianity. It is reflected in the accounts of Islam too. According to Islam, the Quran was dictated to Muhammad, but only Muhammad has heard the voice that actually spoke the dictated words.

The doctrine of the Trinity, however, explains how we can actually know and encounter the living God. The truth is revealed to us in John's Gospel and in the book of Hebrews.

> In the beginning was the Word, and the Word was with God, and the Word was God. He was with God in the beginning. All things were created through Him, and apart from Him not one thing was created that has been created. Life was in Him, and that life was the light of men. . . . The

> Word became flesh and took up residence among us. We observed His glory, the glory as the One and Only Son from the Father, full of grace and truth.... Indeed, we have all received grace after grace from His fullness, for the law was given through Moses, grace and truth came through Jesus Christ. No one has ever seen God. The One and Only Son—the One who is at the Father's side—He has revealed Him. (John 1:1–4, 14, 16–18)

> Long ago God spoke to the fathers by the prophets at different times and in different ways. In these last days, He has spoken to us by His Son. God has appointed Him heir of all things and made the universe through Him. The Son is the radiance of God's glory and the exact expression of His nature, sustaining all things by His powerful word. After making purification for sins, He sat down at the right hand of the Majesty on high. (Heb 1:1–3)

Both of these passages teach us that we can know God. This Christian truth is based on the belief that Jesus is God (Mark 12:35–36; John 8:19; 10:30; 14:8–10).

Just because we can affirm that Jesus is God and his coming to us reveals to us that God is triune, it does not mean that we have a full understanding of what it means for God to be triune. We don't have any examples in our world that illustrate perfectly this doctrine of the Trinity. It is a mystery. We don't have to understand the Trinity to affirm it. It should not surprise us that we don't fully understand it. Isaiah says, "'My thoughts are not your thoughts, and your ways are not My ways.' This is the LORD's declaration. 'For as heaven is higher than earth, so My ways are higher than your ways, and My thoughts than your thoughts'" (55:8–9). Yet, we should remember that just because we don't understand it fully, that does not mean it is incoherent to believe it.

Conclusion: Be Careful with the Question

"Do you believe in God?" We must be careful with this question. We are so accustomed to answering yes that we forget that not all concepts of *who* God is are the same. The Christian doctrine of the Trinity does not fit the mold of any other religion's understanding of God. We must affirm what the Bible affirms about who God is.

Islam says that Allah is not a Father and that there is no divine Son. Islam teaches that Muhammad is the final prophet and that the revelation he received is the authoritative account of Allah's identity. To engage Islam in a missionary encounter, we must be specific about the God we proclaim. The doctrine of the Trinity is the very foundation of the gospel and the basis for claiming that God is good, gracious, and loving toward his people. This doctrine is not irrelevant; it is crucial to our witness to our Muslim neighbors.

Reflection Questions

1. Why is the question, "Do Christians and Muslims worship the same God?" an unhelpful question?
2. How can you begin to explain the difference between Allah and the God of the Bible, using fatherhood as a starting point?
3. Remembering Stetzer's point that we should let Muslims speak for themselves, and understanding how most Muslims believe wrongly about our belief in the Trinity, how might you be able to dispel misconceptions about the Trinity?
4. How is monotheism a bridge to Muslims, and how might you use the bridge of monotheism to engage your neighbor?
5. How would a clear understanding of the Trinity reshape the way you pray for your Muslim neighbors?

6

What Does the Quran Say About Fighting Non-Muslims?

Ayman Ibrahim

Since the terrorist attacks of September 11, 2001, many people in North America have questioned whether terrorism and violence truly reflect the teaching of Islam. Many asked: Does al-Qaeda represent "true Islam"?

With the emergence of ISIS, the same question has resurfaced. Are these violent attacks on innocent civilians consistent with the teaching of Muhammad and the Quran? While many Muslim enthusiasts defend their faith, affirming Islam as a religion of peace as evidenced by multitudes of peaceable Muslims, suspicion and skepticism flourish in the West regarding the nature of violence in Islam.

The answer to the question raised by this chapter is not as straightforward as we might wish. Islam is not a monolithic religion, and so, just as with Christianity, how its teachings are interpreted and applied by one or more of its followers varies from one Islamic community to the next and does not necessarily represent the true faith and practice of the religion as a whole. Therefore, we should acknowledge that the teaching on violence in Islamic sacred texts is disputed even among Muslims. If you were to show the same sacred passage to an average American Muslim in Dearborn, Michigan, and a well-educated scholar of Islamic law in Riyadh, Saudi Arabia, you would probably end up confused at the way they individually interpret the validity of the text and its precedents.

Let me provide a true story. In Texas in 2009, I met with an Iraqi Muslim scholar and former imam (a prayer leader in a mosque) in Baghdad who had recently moved as a refugee to the United States. After we became friends, I asked him what he thought about verse 9:29 of the Quran, which states,"Fight against those who (1) believe not in Allah, (2) nor in the Last Day, (3) nor forbid that which has been forbidden by Allah and His Messenger (4) and those who acknowledge not the religion of truth [i.e., Islam] among the people of the Scripture [i.e., Jews and Christians], until they pay the Jizyah with willing submission, and feel themselves subdued."

At first he was surprised that I knew parts of the Quran. Then, because I did not want to put him in a difficult spot, I told him to think about it and let me know his thoughts later. In the following week, while we were meeting to drink tea, the imam initiated the conversation, saying: "I have an answer about the verse you mentioned. This verse does not apply anymore; it was for the first generation of Muslims and has nothing to do with today's world." While his answer was shocking, it should be noted clearly that many Muslim jurists and scholars, even in the West, would disagree with this man regarding his views of the sacred text. (Some time later, after reading the Sermon on the Mount, this former imam became a follower of Christ.)

Some of the Muslims you encounter may be unclear on what their religion teaches. So a good place to start is to investigate what the most sacred texts in Islam—the Quran and the sayings of Muhammad (known as the *hadith*)—communicate about fighting non-Muslims.

This chapter seeks not only to discuss the complex issue of violence in Islam; we will examine Islam's authoritative texts to discover what they teach on this topic. In addition, we will study the term *jihad* as found in the Arabic translation of the New Testament, to contrast it with the description found in Islam's scripture. Our investigation will help you understand how Muslims think about this topic and prepare you to love them even as religiously motivated violence escalates around the world and in our own country.

Violence in the Hadith

In AD 810, in a city called Bukhara in present-day Uzbekistan, a very important Islamic figure was born, Muhammad ibn Ishmael. Because he was born in Bukhara (located some 2,500 miles from Mecca), he became known as Imam Bukhari. Even though he was born almost two centuries after Muhammad's death and Arabic was not his mother tongue, Bukhari became well-known among Sunni Muslims as the collector of the *sahih* (authentic) sayings and deeds of Muhammad, the hadith. He claimed to have spent more than sixteen years examining hundreds of thousands of accounts attributed to Muhammad, of which only 7,000 or so he deemed as reliable. Bukhari then compiled all the sayings into a series of volumes. Each volume includes several chapters (or books), organized under titles he chose, and each chapter contains a set of sayings arranged by topics. Some of the topics are: Prayer, Menstrual Periods, Prostration, Funerals, Freeing Slaves, Jihad, Military Expeditions, Inheritance Laws, and Punishment Laws.

Under the title "Jihad and Fighting for the Cause of Allah," Bukhari lists various sayings attributed to Muhammad that seem to encourage Muslims to wage war for Allah's cause. In one hadith, Muhammad states, "I have been ordered to fight with the people till they say, 'None has the right to be worshipped but Allah.'" He also says, "Know that Paradise is under the shades of swords," and "He who prepares a Ghazi [fighter] going in Allah's Cause is given a reward equal to that of a fighter." When a believer asked

Muhammad, "Who is the best among the people?" he answered, "A believer who strives his utmost [i.e., practices *jihad*] in Allah's Cause with his life and property." This is also reflected in another hadith, in which Muhammad says, "A single endeavor [of fighting] in Allah's Cause in the forenoon or in the afternoon is better than the world and whatever is in it." Striving with one's life suggests giving one's own life in Allah's cause.

In addition to the theme of fighting, Bukhari also emphasizes Muhammad's teaching on the reward of martyrdom for the sake of Allah. Muhammad was taken in a dream "into a better and superior house, better of which [he had] never seen." When Muhammad asked about this exceptional house, he was told, "This house is the house of martyrs." In regards to fighting Jews in particular, Bukhari reports that Muhammad said, "You [Muslims] will fight with the Jews until some of them will hide behind stones. The stones will [betray them] saying . . . 'There is a Jew hiding behind me; so kill him.'" When Muhammad fought the Jews, he told them: "Embrace Islam and you will be safe."

These sayings are all from one chapter in Bukhari's voluminous collection of Muhammad's authentic sayings and trustworthy deeds. Of course Muslims, as diverse as they are, do not approach, treat, or interpret these sayings exactly alike. In fact, it is safe to assume that some nominal Muslims have never read or heard some of these statements. However, there are at least two major interpretations of such prophetic sayings.

Traditional Muslim interpretations tend to take these sayings literally and adhere to Muhammad's words precisely, seeking to imitate his example to the letter. Others, however, in an attempt to present Islam in a multi-religious context, stress that these sayings do not *necessarily* apply today; one does not need to interpret them literally in contemporary societies, especially where certain forms of Islamic sharia are not applied or where Muslims are not in power. So while *jihad* literally means "striving," the alternative interpreters often consider passages referring to *jihad* as indicating struggle rather than the sense of fighting against someone or something.

Obviously, the existence of these sometimes contradictory interpretive camps confuse Muslims and non-Muslims. While non-Muslims are in no position to decide which Islamic interpretation is right for their Muslim neighbors, it could be argued that some interpretations are more faithful to the sacred ancient texts than others.

In this short chapter, my main emphasis will not be directed to Muhammad's sayings—considered the second most important sacred text in Islam—even though they are considered by Muslims to be authoritative. I intend to focus instead on the most sacred text in Islam, the Quran. What does it say about *jihad* and fighting non-Muslims? What are the words it uses to denote—and by some interpretations, support—violence, particularly against non-Muslims?

Fighting in the Quran

There are two main terms used in the Quran in relation to fighting non-Muslims: *jihad* and *qital*. The terms occur in different forms more than 120 times in Islam's scripture. The word *jihad* in its verbal form means "to strive, struggle, make every effort, labor," and in connection with confronting an enemy, it means fighting and striving for Allah's cause. Among Muslims, *jihad* has various meanings, but *qital* solely means fighting.[1]

The imperative form of *jihad* occurs in the Quran in singular and plural forms. Some of these occurrences have no direct link to fighting.

---

[1] The material on *jihad* and *qital* in the remainder of this chapter is adapted from my dissertation and from Ayman S. Ibrahim, *The Stated Motivations for the Early Islamic Expansion (622–641): A Critical Revision of Muslims' Traditional Portrayal of the Arab Raids and Conquests* (New York: Peter Lang, 2017). Used by permission.

> Do you suppose that you would enter paradise, while Allah has not yet ascertained those of you who have waged *jihad* and not ascertained the steadfast? (QS 3:142)

> Wage *jihad* for the sake of Allah, a *jihad* which is worthy of Him. (QS 22:78)

> Whoever strives [in *jihad*], strives only for his own sake. (QS 29:6)

> If [your parents] urge you [in *jihad*] to ascribe to Me as partner that of which you have no knowledge, then do not obey them. (QS 29:8; similarly, QS 31:15)

> As for those who strive [in *jihad*] in Us, We shall surely guide them in Our ways. (QS 29:69)

Moreover, the Quran uses a form of *jihad* five other times (QS 5:53; 6:109; 16:38; 24:53; 35:42) with no direct relation to waging wars. In a sense, *jihad* here denotes some sort of striving achieved by Muslims for Allah's cause or in Allah's path.

Other verses seem to refer to both struggle in wars and fighting against infidels and polytheists (among others).

> O Prophet! Wage *jihad* against the faithless and the hypocrites, and be severe with them. Their refuge shall be hell, and it is an evil destination. (QS 9:73; cf. QS 66:9; 9:81)

> Do not obey the faithless, but wage against them a great *jihad* with it. (QS 25:52)

> The faithful are only those who have attained faith in Allah and His Apostle and then have never doubted, and who wage *jihad* with their possessions and their persons in the way of Allah. It is they who are the truthful (QS 49:15; cf. QS 61:11).

> Allah has graced [or favored] those who wage *jihad* with their possessions and their persons by a degree over those who sit back [at home]. (QS 4:95; cf. QS 57:10)

The final verse listed compares those who wage *jihad* as they go to war with those who sit at home. Striving with oneself is preferred over staying at home, according to the Quran. To wage *jihad* with your possessions and yourself, some believe, suggests marching to war for Allah's sake.

The Quran also compares those who give away their "possessions and . . . persons [selves]" to those who do not do so. Allah assigns those who wage *jihad* a higher status: "Those who have believed and migrated, and waged *jihad* in the way of Allah with their possessions and persons have a greater rank near Allah, and it is they who are the triumphant" (QS 9:20).

Verse 9:20 presents three phases in a Muslim's life: (1) believing in Muhammad's message, (2) emigrating with him, and (3) striving with one's possessions and self for the cause of Allah. Muslims who are willing to sacrifice their lives and possessions for the sake of Allah are in a better spiritual rank.

A strict interpretation of this passage believes that *jihad* here cannot mean only to live a pious life—it refers to earning a higher rank by defending Allah against infidels. Believers are encouraged to seek higher ranks near Allah by giving not only their possessions but also their lives in wars. This verse promises ranks based on *qital*, while QS 4:95 refers to ranks based on *jihad*, thus reflecting a link between the two terms. Furthermore, consider QS 9:10–17, especially verse 14, which reads "fight them" or "make war on them." Meanwhile, verse 16 refers to those who wage *jihad*.

Qital in the Quran speaks to confrontation and fighting in battles. *Jihad* and *qital* do overlap at times, as we've seen, but we cannot treat them as synonymous because *jihad* does not only mean physical confrontation and combat.

A direct link between *jihad* and *qital* can be traced in some verses. The Quran refers to the *jihad* that is for Allah's sake in QS 2:218; 3:35; 5:54; 8:72, 74; 9:19, 24, 41; 49:15; 60:1; and 61:11, and to *qital* for Allah's sake in QS 2:154, 190, 244, 246; 3:13, 146, 157, 169; 4:74–76, 84; 9:111; 61:4; and 73:20. "Fighting" in QS 2:190, 244, 246 matches "waging *jihad*" in QS 8:72; 9:88; and 49:15. *Qital* is then one meaning of *jihad*.

The command of *qital* occurs in thirty-nine verses in the Quran. Muslims are to fight infidels (QS 8:38–39; 9:12, 123; 48:22), polytheists (QS 9:17, 36), a group called "the People of the Book" (presumably Christians and Jews; QS 9:29), and even a group that transgresses among the Believers (QS 49:9). Fighting non-Muslims is only executed for the sake of Allah, and Muslims should never initiate the attack (QS 2:190). However, Muhammad exhorts his followers to fight (QS 8:65), as fighting is ordained by Allah (QS 2:216). If Muslims are killed in battles, it is for Allah's cause and they are actually alive with him (QS 2:154; 3:169; see also QS 3:195). As they fight, Muslims are actually purchasing the life to come and selling this life (QS 4:74). In fighting the infidels, Muslims are instructed to slay them everywhere they are found (QS 4:89). Doing so is actually according to Allah's will, and he is the one who achieves the slaying himself (QS 8:17).

Qital in the Quran specifically denotes the armed holy war for Allah's cause. While *jihad* and *qital* are not synonymous, they overlap in one aspect: *qital* corresponds to the armed version of *jihad*.

Jihad between the Bible and the Quran

With the rise of ISIS, Boko Haram, and al-Shabaab, as well as al-Qaeda, certain Arabic words have found their way into the English dictionary. For example, *jihad* has become well-known among English speakers after extensive use by various media to describe the militant or terroristic activities of religious enthusiasts, particularly those who self-identify as Muslims. The term is commonly used to refer to Islamic holy war waged against non-Muslims. The Arabic noun *jihadi* is typically applied to a person who executes an act of *jihad*—usually a terrorist attack—under the banner of Islam.

Now that we have studied *jihad* in the Quran, it is important to understand how the word is used in the Arabic translation of the Bible.

The Arabic Bible, particularly the New Testament, uses the term or its derivatives several times in translating the Greek verbs *agōnizomai* and *athleō*. *Jihad*, as an Arabic term, appears some nine times in the Bible, whether in verbal or nominal forms—all in the New Testament, according to the Van Dyck Standard Translation. *Jihad* reflects the personal striving (Gk. *agōnizomai*) to enter the narrow gate of God's kingdom (Luke 13:24). Jesus states that since his kingdom is not an earthly one, his followers must not fight (Gk. *agōnizomai*) to protect him from those who oppose him (John 18:36). This is echoed in Eph 6:12, where the apostle Paul affirms that "our battle [or wrestling] is not against flesh and blood, but against . . . spiritual forces of evil in the heavens." Paul actually used the same term in connection with spiritual training, emphasizing that believers need to make every effort (Gk. *agōnizomai*) at self-control, in the same way that a boxer works to make his body his slave (1 Cor 9:24–27). The apostle also uses a participle of *jihad* to depict his diligent endeavor to preach God's good news, and to teach and warn people using the wisdom of God (Col 1:29).

Jihad also refers to the effort expended in praying earnestly and fervently. Epaphras, a bondservant of Christ, prays earnestly (Gk. *agōnizomai*) that the Colossian believers will be strengthened and perfected by God (Col 4:12). Paul, in his last years as a prisoner because of his gospel preaching, declares that he has kept the faith while striving (Gk. *agōnizomai*) to finish the spiritual race. He has remained faithful in and committed to preaching the gospel of Christ (2 Tim 4:7). He thus instructs Timothy to endure suffering as a good soldier of Christ and as an athlete who strives (Gk. *athleō*) to win the heavenly reward (2 Tim 2:5). Paul further calls Timothy to strive to fight the good spiritual fight, preserving the authenticity of the true faith, holding tightly to eternal life, and preaching and proclaiming the good confession of faith in the presence of many witnesses (1 Tim 6:12).

Thus, *jihad* in the Arabic New Testament signifies a personal effort to practice self-control, prevailing against one's own desires—it is a call to fight to overcome oneself. The word also denotes striving to bring the good news of Christ to everyone near and far, proclaiming and preserving the genuineness and purity of the Christian faith. *Jihad* is encouraged in prayer as believers intercede fervently for the work of God in the life of his church. It is never used in direct reference to violence against enemies. Since Jesus Christ's kingdom is not an earthly one, his followers do not need to resort to physical fighting as a form of *jihad* for him.

The Quran, on the other hand, uses the term to reflect the efforts one ought to make to enter paradise, as well as stirring its believers to go to physical battle against non-Muslims for the sake of Allah and his cause. This is not surprising, however, when you consider the difference in Christian and Muslim understanding of access to God's eternal kingdom, and specifically the Muslim belief that works on behalf of Allah are a means of making oneself acceptable to him.

Conclusion

So does the Quran encourage violence against non-Muslims? The answer is "yes and no." Not all Muslims—not even most them—want to harm you. Yet we are not truthful if we claim there is no Islamic problem with violence. The Quran and Muhammad's hadith contain precise statements that call for violence against non-Muslims. People need to come to terms with what the sacred Muslim texts say. However, because there is severe dissonance in the Muslim community regarding this issue, especially with the brutal deeds propagated by ISIS, it is no wonder that, in the midst of Muslim confusion, Christians struggle to make sense of the Islamic stance on violence.

As we wait in hope for Muslims to reinterpret their sacred texts to support religious freedom and mutual coexistence, we cannot be silent. We have the gospel of hope, which we believe is needed by every Muslim who has moved into our communities. What's more, we are a people who believe that the advance of the gospel and the glory of God is more important than any violence we might face.

It is true that most Muslims living in North America are unlikely to want to bring you harm. Yet even when engaging those who might intend harm, we have confidence in the gospel. We have already died to ourselves as we believed the gospel. Our lives are not our own. We have been shaped by the peace that Christ offers, and we are called to reflect that peace to the world. We need to reflect the Prince of Peace to the multitude of Muslims in our neighborhoods and beyond.

Reflection Questions

1. What are the primary two interpretations of the word *jihad*?
2. How might you have misunderstood *jihad* in the past?
3. What does the Arabic translation of the New Testament have to say about *jihad*?
4. How does the New Testament usage of *jihad* vary from the Quranic use?
5. How might you engage in a conversation with a Muslim neighbor about the similarities and differences between *jihad* in the New Testament and the Quran?

7

Do Muslims Want to Overtake America's Political Structure and Institute Sharia Law?

Bob Roberts

Are most Muslims living in America intent on establishing sharia law in the United States? No, most Muslims do not want to overtake US political structure and institute sharia law. But many American Christians are unsure this is the case.

LifeWay Research surveyed 1,000 American pastors and 1,000 American citizens about their views on Islam's impact on society. In February 2015, the published results revealed that

- 43 percent of Americans think true Islam creates a peaceful society
- 61 percent of American Protestant pastors disagree that Islam is fundamentally peaceful.
- 51 percent of evangelical pastors believe that ISIS is a true indication of what Islam looks like when Islam controls a society

- 36 percent of mainline pastors would agree that ISIS is a true indication of what Islam looks like when Islam controls a society
- 27 percent of Americans would say ISIS is a true indication of what Islam looks like when Islam controls a society
- 37 percent of Americans worry about sharia law being applied in the United States.[1]

The report indicates that a significant number of Americans are concerned that sharia may be applied in the United States. Consequently, as the number of Muslims moving into our town and cities increases, this concern will likely increase.

I have heard some American Christians say that Muslims plan to take over the American political system and conform it to sharia law as soon as they have a majority in the United States. I do not deny that there are some Islamic extremists who want to take over America's political structure in addition to the entire world. Ignoring that fact would be naïve. But when compared to the total global Muslim population, extremists are a very small minority. When it comes to North America, the facts are pretty clear; many, if not most, Muslims who immigrate here come to escape the extreme ways that sharia is applied in certain areas of the world. So, while the social impact of Islam on the United States is important for us to consider, as Christians we cannot allow fear to control us. We need to develop a hospitable empathy for those seeking to live in a land not oppressed by sharia.

What Is Sharia?

Apart from terrorist extremists, nothing incites fear among non-Muslims in America like the term *sharia* and its threat to the

[1] Bob Smietana, "One in Three Americans Worry about Sharia Law Being Applied in America," Lifeway Research, February 11, 2015, https://lifewayresearch.com/2015/02/11/1-in-3-americans-worry-about-sharia-law-being-applied-in-america/.

Constitution. Yet when asked, those who cite sharia as a reason for refusing immigrants and refugees from Muslim countries generally cannot define it. They point to acts such as hands being cut off for stealing, women being stoned for adultery, or Muslims being executed for changing religions. This reflects a limited and biased understanding of sharia law.

What is sharia? Simply defined, sharia is "the fundamental religious concept of Islam, namely, its law."[2] The term itself means the "path" or "way" leading to the watering place. It is more comprehensive than most other laws in that it is a way of life, both publicly and privately, for living under Islam. Sharia does not merely give prescriptions and prohibitions; it also deals with issues of ethics and conscience, and how life should be lived as informed by Allah. Some laws classify acts as praiseworthy, where a person deserves divine favor for doing them or disfavor for failing to do them. Other laws classify acts as morally corrupt, such that an individual deserves divine favor for avoiding them and disfavor for doing them. Sharia deals with all aspects of life: politics, economics, banking, business law, contract law, sexuality, and social issues. It is not a strict set of laws, but a comprehensive code of behavior that embraces both private and public activities.[3]

---

[2] Noel James Coulson, "Sharīʿah," *Encyclopædia Britannica*, updated April 13, 2018, https://www.britannica.com/topic/Shariah.

[3] Sayyid Qutb, *The Islamic Concept and Its Characteristics* (n.p.: American Trust Publications, 1992). Page 19 of "Comprehensiveness," uploaded to Scribd by Ibn Sadiq (https://www.scribd.com/document/27798540/Comprehensiveness), describes the Islamic notion of comprehensiveness: "This comprehensiveness of the Islamic concept in all its forms . . . protects man from turning to anyone other than Allah, in any condition or at any moment, and protects him from accepting the domination of anyone who does not derive his authority from Allah within the limits of His shari'ah (Divine Law) in any field of life. Command, Dominion, and Authority belong to Allah alone, not merely in the sphere of 'worship,' or only in some other sphere, but in all spheres, in this life and in the life of the Hereafter, in the heavens and on earth,

The first Muslim community was established by the Prophet Muhammad in Medina in AD 622. He would personally rule on all issues of life in the community in a sort of ad hoc manner. Those who came after him did the same. In many ways, sharia is the combination of Arabian customs at the time of Muhammad's law with some Jewish law. The Quran was not as much a comprehensive legal system as it was a code of conduct. Only eighty verses deal with legal issues in the entire Quran.

One cannot go out and purchase a copy of the sharia law. It is not a codified book of laws. If it were, you would find one form of Islam practiced in all fifty-seven Muslim-majority nations. Instead, you find fifty-seven different varieties of Islam from Saudi Arabia to Turkey. The law cannot be altered, but imams exercise a certain freedom in their interpretation of it, which is called *fiqh*. Thus, there are many interpretations of sharia. Some are certainly more strict and conservative, and many are less so.

With the formation of the Umayyad dynasty in AD 661, which governed a vast empire from Damascus, a much broader legal system was necessary. *Qadis*, or judges, were appointed in provinces and districts. Varied interpretations were found among the districts, and various fraternities banded together to create a consistent approach. As the Abbasid rulers came to power, desiring to build a true Islamic state and society, these schools of law marked the beginning of Islamic jurisprudence.

The two most important early schools of thought were the Malikis in Medina and the Hanafis in al-Kufa, named after two outstanding Muslim scholars. Because their contexts were different and there was freedom of interpretation, a deep conflict of juristic principles between the schools emerged. The Malikis wanted things derived only from the Quran, while the Hanifis were free to use their

---

in the visible and in the unseen worlds, in prayer and in action, and this is true for every soul in its every movement, every step, and every direction."

reason. To bring unity, the famous jurist al-Shafi (d. AD 820) used four roots of Islamic law to determine the law and rulings. Sharia, as it was known, became a system based on these four roots.

First, it was based on the Quran. Next, it was based on the hadith (interpretations of the Quran and sayings of the prophet) and the Sunna. In the Sunna, you could learn about the example, actions, and words of the prophet Muhammad. The third root was called "consensus." Muslims believe that Allah would never allow his community to live unanimously in error. The result was judges and scholars who would come together to discuss rulings and positions. These rulings and positions had to be established by qualified scholars of a particular generation and school. The fourth root was reason and analogy. It did not formally begin to take shape until between the eighth and tenth centuries.

These other schools did not view each other as heretical as much as distinct from one another. Thus, a principled pluralism existed based on the statement by the Prophet Muhammad in which he honored diversity: "Difference of opinion among my community is a sign of the bounty of Allah."

Over time, five schools of thought developed, each with its own interpretation of sharia law. The four major schools in Sunni Islam are Hanafi, Maliki, Shāfi'ī and Ḥanbalī. There is only one major school of thought in Shi'a Islam, which is Ja'fari. Concerning sharia, these schools agree on topics explicitly covered in the Quran, but they differ on matters not covered in the Quran.

The Ḥanbalī school takes the most traditionalist interpretive approach, meaning that they focus on a literal reading and application of the original source materials, mainly the Quran and the Sunna. This school spawned the Wahabi and Salafi branches of Islam and is embraced by groups such as the Taliban and by Saudi Arabia. The Hanafi school is known to take a more progressive interpretive approach, focusing more on reason and analogy. It is dominant among Sunnis in central Asia, Egypt, Pakistan, India, China, Turkey, the Balkans, and the Caucasus. The Maliki school is dominant in North Africa; and the Shafi'i school in Indonesia, Malaysia, Brunei Darussalam, and Yemen. The Ja'fari school from Shi'a Islam is practiced mostly in Iran.[4]

Sharia law is broken into two primary sections. The first section would be the Five Pillars of Islam, or acts of worship, which are called *ibadat*:

1. *Shahadah*, or Affirmation: "There is no God except Allah, and Muhammad is his messenger." Whenever a person says this confession three times and means it, he or she becomes a Muslim.
2. *Salah*: prayer five times a day
3. *Sawm* during Ramadan: fasts
4. *Zakat*: giving to charities
5. *Hajj*: pilgrimage to Mecca

The second section of sharia deals with human interaction, or *al-mu'amalat*, which includes laws governing the following:

1. financial transactions
2. endowments
3. laws of inheritance
4. marriage, divorce, and child custody
5. foods and drinks (including ritual slaughtering and hunting)
6. penal punishments
7. warfare and peace
8. judicial matters (including witnesses and forms of evidence)

Within sharia, there are three categories of crime: *oisas, tazir*, and *hudud*. *Oisas* are crimes against Muslims where retaliation is

[4] Toni Johnson and Mohammed Aly Sergie, "Islam: Governing under Sharia," Council on Foreign Relations, July 25, 2014, http://www.cfr.org/religion/islam-governing-under-sharia/p8034http://www.cfr.org/religion/islam-governing-under-sharia/p8034.

permissible. *Tazir* is a crime against a Muslim or non-Muslim, and a Muslim judge determines the appropriate sentencing. *Hudud* are the greatest crimes, for they are against God.

Within these types of crimes, some illegal acts have predetermined punishments tied to them. Apostasy and highway robbery are punishable by death. The sentence for theft is amputation of the hand. For the married offender in an extramarital sexual relationship, the penalty is death by stoning. If unmarried, the person will be lashed 100 times. For the unproven accusation of being unchaste and drinking alcohol, eighty lashes are administered. Outside of these crimes, the prosecution and punishment of offenses lies within the discretion of the executive or the court.

While all of these punishments sound severe, this is a realm where interpretation comes into play. Ali Mazrui of the Institute of Global Cultural Studies stated in a *Voice of America* interview, "These [harsh] punishments remain on the books in some countries, but lesser penalties are often considered sufficient." Extremist groups, such as al-Qaeda and ISIS, apply the *hudud* punishments, though the frequency of their application across Islamic history is debatable. Some people feel justified taking the law into their own hands, resulting in vigilante justice. Honor killings—murders committed in retaliation for bringing dishonor on one's family—are a worldwide problem. These incidents, and others, elicit much controversy among Muslims. There is much debate over what the Quran sanctions and what practices were pulled from local customs that predate Islam.[5]

Sharia Is Not Universally Applied

In global Islam, there is no universal position on the appropriate role of sharia in governing the laws of a country. In 2015, the Pew

[5] For further study, see Joseph Schacht, *The Origins of Muhammadan Jurisprudence* (Oxford: Clarendon Press, 1959); see also Noel James Coulson, *A History of Islamic Law* (Edinburgh: Edinburgh University Press, 1964).

Foundation surveyed Muslims from the ten most populated countries to learn about their perspective on whether the Quran should influence their nation's law. The results—which revealed significantly differing opinions among Muslims—were illuminating in light of the prevailing belief among Americans that Muslims are unanimous on this issue. Half of the population in Pakistan, the Palestine territories, Jordan, Malaysia, and Senegal affirmed that their country should strictly follow the Quran. However, in Burkina Faso, Turkey, Lebanon, and Indonesia, less than 25 percent agreed.[6]

Even within a country, a range of views on this topic exists. In Jordan, 54 percent of survey respondents said the Quran should be followed strictly. However, 38 percent said the country's laws should follow the values and principles of the Quran but not follow the Quran strictly, and 7 percent responded that the laws should not be influenced in any way by the Quran. In six of the ten countries surveyed, people with at least a secondary education were more likely to say the national law should not be influenced by the Quran.[7]

The impact of Western civilization on Muslim society through colonialism cannot be underestimated in areas such as civil society, commercial transactions, and criminal law. The result has been that the criminal and general civil law of sharia was abandoned in most Muslim countries. Sharia was replaced by new legal codes based on European models, with a new system of secular tribunals to apply them. Thus, Muslim majority nations now face the challenge of how to implement sharia in a modern context.

In most Islamic-majority nations, sharia family law is expressed in modern codes and statutory legislation. Most countries now also have appellate jurisdictions. In places such as Egypt and Tunisia, the

---

[6] Jacob Pouster, "The Divide over Islam and National Laws in the Muslim World," Pew Research Center, April 27, 2016, http://www.pewglobal.org/2016/04/27/the-divide-over-islam-and-national-laws-in-the-muslim-world.

[7] Pouster.

separate sharia courts do not exist anymore. Sharia law is administered through a unified system of national courts.[8] There have been many attempts at reform, including various views of interpretation of how to bring Islamic law and modern realities closer together. But there have been, and will continue to be, challenges. Traditionalists remain resistant to reinterpreting the basic texts of divine revelation.[9]

Much of the controversy around sharia and its supposed implementation in the United States is clouded with misunderstanding. Previously in this book, Ed Stetzer warned, "To find out what is important to Muslims, do not watch biased news reports—from liberal or conservative media." What should we do? We should talk to people and hear what they have to say.

Listening to Those We Seek to Reach

This chapter challenges us to think rightly about Islam and the potential that Muslim migration may have on North American society. As we consider these questions, we must remember that while we face the uncertainty of change, we do so with a mission. We are called to proclaim the gospel to all peoples. Gospel conversations require us to listen carefully to those we are seeking to reach so we can know how they see and understand the world. To do this, we must allow followers of Islam to speak for themselves. When we assume we understand what other people feel, believe,

[8] See, for example, Mohamed S. E. Abdel Wahab, "UPDATE: An Overview of the Egyptian Legal System and Legal Research," GlobaLex, October 2012, http://www.nyulawglobal.org/globalex/Egypt1.html.

[9] Nasr Abu Zayd, *Reformation of Islamic Thought: A Critical Historical Analysis* (Amsterdam: Amsterdam University Press, 2006). See also Fazlur Rahman, *Islam and Modernity: Transformation of an Intellectual Tradition* (Chicago: University of Chicago Press, 1982).

and think—we enter conversations not needing to understand but intending to teach.

Over the years, I've had a number of experiences and conversations that have helped me understand this issue better. I am friends with several Muslim scholars and imams whom I recently saw at a meeting. In preparation for writing this chapter, I asked them whether the majority of Muslims living in the United States want sharia law adopted into the legal system. Without exception, each one of them said they moved to the United States because of the freedoms enjoyed by the people who live here. They did not want to lose those freedoms.

Their follow-up question helped clarify this issue even further. They asked, "Bob, what would it look like if sharia law took over the United States political system? Which country has implemented sharia like that?" With their question, they made an important point. Sharia is a bit of an ambiguous concept that is applied in a variety of ways across the world. The implementation of sharia is dependent on various streams of translation and interpretation in the Muslim world. As a result, there is not a one-size-fits-all model for how to implement sharia law in the Muslim world. It is not a stretch to say that sharia looks different for each of the fifty-seven Muslim-majority nations in the world. This fact suggests that there is not a vast conspiracy to implement a specific political system anywhere, let alone the United States.

My next experience happened a few years ago when I had the privilege of joining a group of pastors in Washington, DC, who are a part of my own conservative evangelical denomination. We sat down with Sayid Saad, who helped start the Islamic Association of North America in the 1960s and is now in charge of interfaith engagement. He shared with us that he came to the United States of America so that his daughters could enjoy opportunities they would not have had if they remained in the Middle East. Sayid affirmed his love for America and his support for our way of life.

Further, he pointed out that his understanding of sharia teaches Muslims that they are expected to support the laws of the country they call home, and that they are called to be responsible citizens wherever they live.

I'll share one last example. For the past six years, I've been friends with Imam Zia, who leads the Irving Islamic Center in the Dallas, Texas, area. Four years ago, Imam Zia and three other imams decided to start an Islamic mediation center so they could give sharia-based, theological rulings on business or family matters, such as divorce or child custody. Their mission is to provide "mediation and non-binding arbitration that adheres to Islamic principles in the Muslim community." Since these decisions are non-binding, they can also be taken to the appropriate civil court if legal entanglements are involved. In other words, even after a sharia-based ruling is rendered, those involved still have to live under the laws of the land, and the case can be put before a courtroom judge to be legally confirmed.

This practice is similar to the practice of other religious groups. The Catholic Church has canon law. The Jewish faith has religious rules and practices called *Halakhah*. In Christian circles, we seek to honor Paul's teaching in 1 Cor 6:1–11; thus, Christians have sought to practice biblically based arbitration at times, to settle disputes. In each of these forms of religious "law," a decision, once rendered, still must meet legal requirements. Religious courts or arbitrators cannot create forms of law to be followed outside the bounds of the law of the land.

As an example of the importance of this type of mediation in Muslim communities, Imam Zia explained to me a situation in which women may legally obtain a divorce from their husbands, and yet the husband may refuse to acknowledge the divorce because he believes the divorce is not recognized by their faith. Catholics and some other faith traditions might find themselves in similar scenarios. The acknowledgment of the imams and the rendering of an Islamic judgment would give religious credibility to the woman's decision, thus actually protecting her by allowing her to be divorced yet remain a Muslim in good standing. Imam Zia's mediation center, therefore, serves to protect the rights of women, even though its decisions do not carry the weight of civil law.[10]

Confusing Practice and Growing Concern

Regardless of such efforts by Muslims to live within the United States legal system, a proliferation of fear and misinformation has led to conflict. A sensational website wrote a story on the Islamic mediation center in Irving, asserting that it was a sharia court attempting to subvert American law. People assumed the court was being used to oppress women, when in fact, it was accomplishing just the opposite. Nevertheless, the local mayor learned about the practice through the website and posted a response on Facebook. She declared that the city would not accept any form of sharia court and that she would personally work to block it. Sadly, this mayor never initiated contact with the imams to inquire as to what was actually occurring. The mayor called a private meeting at which she declared that she would introduce a bill into the Texas Legislature opposing sharia law, asserting that Muslims should get behind it. The bill was introduced in the state legislature, but ultimately it failed to pass.

---

[10] Visit Islamictribunal.org for more information about what they do. Mona Siddiqui, "Sharia and the Public Debate," *Political Theology* 9, no. 3 (2008): 262–63, also describes the action of Islamic arbitration from the perspective of the United Kingdom: "Many in the legal profession are aware that Islamic divorce proceedings must be done in the framework of both religious and civil law. However, they are also aware of the dangerous position this leaves women who become victims caught between two legal systems. . . . While some, like the Islamic Sharia Council in London, claim that the majority of their rulings are on divorce and about releasing women from bad or forced marriages, these sharia courts know that their rulings have no basis in law—participants abide by them voluntarily."

This misunderstanding of sharia law by Americans led to an increasing furor and a lack of religious protection for people who might otherwise be vulnerable, in this case, women.

Following sharia for Muslims means much more than the simplistic and often misunderstood definitions that are often articulated in the Western world. Sharia is a way of life for Muslims. If they cannot practice sharia, it means they cannot pray, they cannot eat halal food, they cannot bury their dead, and they cannot be married—each of which exists within sharia law.

Though sharia is far more complex than just legal rulings, there is much misunderstanding and even hysteria associated with Islam in America. Too often this results in people making public statements without fully understanding the issues. Sadly, we allow news pundits and their sensational appeals to determine what we think, what we feel, and how we view sharia. Further, we forget the strength of our political and legal systems. In a country like the United States, any proposed law cannot contradict our governing documents, particularly the Constitution.

I once watched a news program where someone would go up to a Muslim and ask, "Which law is higher, the Constitution or sharia?" If the person answered "Sharia," he or she was condemned by the commentator as a threat to the American way of life. But to do so was inappropriate. The person being interviewed was not allowed to explain his or her answer, and no definition of sharia law was provided. Thus, the answer incited people unnecessarily. If you were to ask most practicing evangelicals whether God's law or man's law is higher, the answer would almost always be God's law, and we would applaud this answer.

Conclusion

There is a deep divide concerning how the West and the Islamic world should live together in modern society. Islamic nations are modernizing, even in how they view the law. I was recently with some of the most influential Muslim imams in America as they visited some leading Christian pastors. The question was asked, "Where in the world can one find the best expression of Islam today that can serve as a model for other Islamic nations?" The answer was the same from all of the imams: "Here in the United States, we are creating the best model of how to live in a pluralistic world."

So, to answer the original question—do Muslims want to overtake America's political system and implement sharia law?—certainly some do, but the vast majority of global Muslims appear to want to live peaceably within the constraints of the political system in which they find themselves. They understand sharia not to be a form of law meant to subjugate everyone regardless of faith, but rather, the way they live their lives as faithful Muslims.

Our calling is to engage all people with the gospel of Jesus Christ. To do this, we have to follow Ed Stetzer's second principle: we have to "talk with and about *individuals*, not generic 'faiths.'" I have tried to model talking with individuals in this chapter. Talking with others to learn from them requires that we ask questions and listen to the answers being shared. A topic such as the implementation of sharia law in the United States can be unsettling. Still, we need to listen to what people are saying and not assume what they think. That's the only way we can build a relationship with them. Without that relationship, it will be hard for them to listen to what we believe about the person and work of Jesus Christ.

Reflection Questions

1. What did you learn about sharia law in this chapter?
2. How has this chapter encouraged you to be hospitable to Muslims in your community?

3. Why are many American Christians fearful of Muslim extremists taking over the country?
4. How does the gospel combat fear of Muslim extremists and sharia?
5. How would you respond if you did encounter a Muslim who believes that sharia law should be implemented in our political system?

PART 3

GREAT COMMISSION OPPORTUNITIES

8

Discovering the Missional Opportunity

Micah Fries

Islam is growing in North America. This fact is essentially unquestioned. How much it is growing and what is fueling its growth, however, are the crucial questions for understanding how Christians should engage the emerging Islamic population in North America.

In chapter 2, Steve Johnson provided a helpful overview of the current state of global Islam and Islam in North America. But what does that mean for the future of Islam in North America? How should this view of the future shape how we engage the growing number of Muslims whom God is bringing to our communities?

I have a number of Muslim friends, some of them converts to Islam. One friend was born and raised in a Catholic family on the East Coast, but converted to Islam as a young man. Now he is committed to Islam and diligently practices his faith. Many Christians think that my friend's story reflects how Islam is growing in North America. People believe that when nominal Christianity meets passionate Islamic faith, conversion to Islam is the result.

While there seems to be much fear about Islam growing through proselytization, the data simply does not support that concern. Islam is growing in North America, but the growth is neither dramatic, nor is it a reflection of significant numbers of Americans converting to Islam. The significant growth of Islam results from Muslims immigrating to North America, and the remainder of the growth results from the biological expansion of Muslim families: Islam is growing in North America because of immigration and birth rates. This reality should help shape the way Christians understand their Muslim neighbors, and also how we ought to engage them as people created in God's image.

I have two other Muslim friends living in North America, and their stories actually reflect what is taking place. Both of these friends are from Iraq—one from central Iraq, and the other from the northern part of the country. As a result of the escalating violence in their hometowns, and after experiencing that violence themselves (losing friends and family and suffering personal harm), they applied for asylum to the United States as refugees. They both moved to America with their wives and children. Migrating to the United States did not solve all their problems. They face challenges and hardships as they settle in their homes. They struggle to find and keep stable jobs to financially provide for their families. They struggle to learn English. They struggle to make friends in a culture that is increasingly hostile toward refugees, particularly from Islamic countries.

If we are going to engage Muslims, we need to understand what is happening in their community. First, we must understand the cause of the projected growth of Muslims.[1] According to Pew Research:

> Just over half of the projected growth of the American Muslim population from 2010 to 2015 is due to immigration. Over the last 20 years, there has been an increase in

[1] This chapter was written at approximately the same time as President Donald Trump's inauguration and executive order concerning refugee resettlement in the United States. Depending on the outcome of those decisions, the data contained in this chapter could shift.

> the number of Muslim immigrants coming to the U.S. The number of Muslim immigrants currently represents about 10% of all legal immigrants arriving in the U.S., and a significantly smaller percentage of unauthorized immigrants.[2]

Muslims make up only a small number of unauthorized or undocumented immigrants. One reason for this is the "logistics" of arriving in the United States. Nearly all Muslim immigrants have to enter the United States through airports, whereas a larger number of undocumented immigrants are able to walk across the southern border.

Between immigration and the higher birth rate among Muslim populations,[3] nearly all of the growth can be explained. Nevertheless, we want to know how many people in the United States are converting to Islam. The easy answer is, very few. This might surprise most Americans, but according to recent data, the number of those who are embracing Islam is roughly equivalent to the number of those who are leaving the Muslim faith. The net gain through proselytizing is zero. Pew Research reports, "About one-in-five American Muslim adults were raised in a different faith or none at all. At the same time, a similar number of people who were raised Muslim no longer identify with the faith."[4]

On a popular website, I recently saw the headline: "Muslim Population in U.S. to Double by 2050." The headline is technically correct, but it leads you to think that Islam will soon overwhelm the United States. Headlines like these are used to strike fear in readers, inciting them to oppose immigrants from Muslim countries. Such insinuations are seemingly successful. Fear does exist in

---

[2] Mohamed, "A New Estimate of the U.S. Muslim Population" (see chap. 1, n. 4).

[3] Pew "Why Muslims Are the World's Fastest-Growing Religious Group," Pew Research Center, April 23, 2015, http://www.pewresearch.org/fact-tank/2015/04/23/why-muslims-are-the-worlds-fastest-growing-religious-group/ft_15-04-23_muslimfertility.

[4] Pew.

America over the growth of Islam, and there is a growing animosity toward Muslims in the United States. As a result, many American Christians are paralyzed when it comes to engaging their Muslim coworkers and neighbors with the gospel.

The statement itself, however, implies something that is wrong. Yes, Islam is growing. Yes, Islam is projected to double in the next few decades. But when the numbers are taken into consideration, only a small percentage of residents in the United States will follow Islam. According to Pew Research, Islam is projected to grow from approximately 1 percent to 2.1 percent of the US population by 2050.[5] This data does reflect a significant increase. However, the current number of Muslims is relatively small, and it will continue to be small even as it doubles in size. I suspect that the vast majority of Americans would be shocked to know that Muslims only make up around 1 percent of the current population in the United States.

While writing this chapter, I polled a number of people to see if they knew the percentage of Muslims in the United States. Most were college-educated, many with seminary degrees and careers in the religious world. Without exception, they gave a much higher number than 1 percent. The concerns about the growth of Islam have seemingly far outpaced its actual size.

Some of the reasons for this growing concern are the media and those who overstate the information for political gain. The most troubling aspect of this situation is that Christians believe the misinformation and respond in fear. The fear stems in part from threats that Christianity will lose its dominant position in the culture. The threat of danger should not be dismissed, because it does exist. It existed in our culture before the current migration of Muslims to the United States. But I contend that false information has inflated the perception of the danger.

---

[5] Mohamed, "A New Estimate of the U.S. Muslim Population."

Migration and Gospel Opportunity

How then should evangelical Christians view the current growth of Islam in America? How should we react to it? Should we view it as a good thing? Or a concern? The immediate answer is that evangelicals should be concerned about the growth because it reflects the potential momentum of Islam, and yet simultaneously we should view it as a great gospel opportunity. While most evangelicals see the missionary opportunity to reach Muslims who have moved to North America, few Christians engage Muslims in gospel conversations.

In a recent research project conducted by LifeWay Research and sponsored by the Evangelical Immigration Table and World Relief, we learn the following:

- Only 21 percent of evangelicals say they have ever been encouraged by their local church to reach out to immigrants in their communities.
- Over 50 percent of evangelicals agree that they are very familiar with what the Bible says about how immigrants should be treated.
- Nearly 75 percent of evangelicals agree that the arrival of immigrants presents a great opportunity to share Jesus Christ.[6]

Less than one-quarter of evangelicals are being encouraged by their churches to reach out to immigrants. Yet more than half of the evangelicals surveyed are confident that they know what the Bible teaches about how to treat immigrants. The disparity between these responses is significant.

Evangelicals are aware of the significant evangelistic opportunity Muslim immigration offers the church. Almost three-quarters

[6] "Evangelical Views on Immigration," LifeWay Research, February 2015, 17–19, http://lifewayresearch.com/wp-content/uploads/2015/03/Evangelical-Views-on-Immigration-Report.pdf.

of evangelical Christians believe the current arrival of immigrants offers a tremendous prospect for gospel advance, but they are not being mobilized to reach out to immigrants in their communities. One of the reasons for this book is that we are convinced that the church cannot afford to miss this gospel opportunity. Pastors and church leaders are called to equip and deploy their members to love and engage their neighbors for the sake of the gospel. This includes their Muslim neighbors.

God's call to share the gospel should be the only reason we need to evangelize Muslims moving into our communities. I fear that political and cultural concerns have eclipsed the biblical mandate to engage others with the gospel. When asked what factors most influenced their convictions on immigration, 10 percent of evangelicals named the Bible and 2 percent named their church. The factors receiving the highest responses were personal relationships with immigrants, opinions of friends and family, and reporting by mass media.

History demonstrates that God has used migration to advance his gospel message among previously resistant people. In *Global Diasporas and Mission*, Jenny Yang points out:

> For Christians who participate in God's redemptive purposes, the migration of people, whether forced or voluntary, should be viewed not as accidental, but as part of God's sovereign plan. God determines the exact times and places where people live "so that they might seek God, and perhaps they might reach out and find him" (Acts 17:27). We are called to "make disciples of all nations" (Matthew 28:19); with immigration, the nations show up on our doorstep. The mission field has crossed our borders and settled into our communities as our coworkers and neighbors.[7]

---

[7] Jenny Hwang Yang, "Immigrants in the USA: A Missional Opportunity," *Global Diasporas and Mission*, ed. Chandler Im and Amos Yong (Eugene, OR: Cascade, 2014), 148.

Christians need to resist being apathetic or unaware of immigration growth in North America. We also need to resist a version of nationalism that suspects anyone who does not give priority to American interests. This ideology becomes even more problematic when American Christians marry nationalism to their religious beliefs.

In a recent journal article in *American Politics Research,* Eric Leon McDaniel, Irfan Nooruddin, and Allyson Faith Shortle argue that when one's American identity is conflated with religious ideals, it negatively impacts one's acceptance of immigrants from different religious backgrounds. Here is a condensed version of their argument:

> When American identity is infused with religious ideals, this will increase the symbolic threat level. . . . These social identity arguments lead us to hypothesize that those high in Christian nationalist leanings should have increasingly negative immigrant attitudes because of the threat they perceive by outside groups that potentially challenge their own values and beliefs. . . . Because of the intertwining of religion and nationalism, immigration threatens their entire Christian national identity by permitting others to alter their exclusive conceptions of what it means to be an American.[8]

Their analysis shows that political ideology and theology can intersect to (negatively) shape one's view of immigrants, which in turn impacts one's (un)willingness to engage immigrants with the gospel. This leads to a place where we Christians view our Muslim neighbors with skepticism and fear rather than as individuals created in the image of God and as possible recipients of God's saving grace.

---

[8] Eric Leon McDaniel, Irfan Nooruddin, and Allyson Faith Shortle, "Divine Boundaries: How Religion Shapes Citizens' Attitudes Toward Immigrants," *American Politics Research* 39 (2011): 213.

The Church's Mission and Muslim Immigration

What do these observations mean for the future of Islam in North America? More significantly, what do these observations mean for the future of Islam in North America as it relates to the church? Allow me to conclude this chapter with a couple of specific thoughts about how we should understand the future of Islam and engage Muslims in North America.

1. Immigration will necessitate relationships between Christians and Muslims.

In an increasingly pluralistic society, Christians have three possible options. We can ignore the increasing pluralism. We can work to reverse the pluralism. Or we can build growing numbers of relationships with those who disagree with us. I fear that many Christians are using the second approach. They are working politically to impede immigration to North America, and they are justifying this action with vague or twisted scriptural support. To slow the growth of pluralism, they seek to protect what it means to be an American.

I would contend, however, that the growing number of diverse religious beliefs and worldviews is an indication of how God is moving, bringing the world to us. I concur with Ed Stetzer and his thoughts about migration and gospel opportunity.

> Immigration puts a face on those we are called to reach, which makes evangelism more complicated.
>
> And as it turns out, many non-Christians—particularly devout people of other religions—are pretty nice once you get to know them! They are not "people over there living in darkness," but they are our neighbors living in our community. . . .
>
> Immigration becomes an evangelistic opportunity when it gives us a love for immigrants as human beings (without caricature) and teaches us to have compassion for

> them (including their spiritual condition), as we would for anyone in need of the gospel.[9]

The emerging cultural changes taking place around immigration cause social and cultural challenges. The messiness of relationships is worth it, though. The church is called to recognize its evangelistic responsibility and opportunity in the midst of these changes. I do not fear growing numbers of people who are different from me, and you should not either. Instead, let us view this as a unique, historical moment that we can steward for God's glory and the common good.

2. Immigration will open doors for gospel engagement among Muslim communities. One of the unintended consequences of immigration is the increased willingness of immigrant communities to consider new and otherwise unwelcome ideologies. This can help pave the way for the introduction of the gospel. Mark Russell and Daniel Ryumugabe discuss this in an article that was originally published in the *Lausanne World Pulse.*

> In Ted Lewellen's work, *The Anthropology of Globalization,* he points out that migrating people often develop a new identity—or at the least have their previous identity significantly altered. Moreover, the current trends of migration have largely eliminated the historical dichotomies (such as rural/urban) and have produced the need to look at things in a more fluid way. Social networks can be borderless due to increases in efficiency and decreases in the cost of transportation and communication technologies. The world is changing and so is the face of migration.[10]

---

[9] Ed Stetzer, "4 Ways (Im)migration Impacts the Mission of the Church," *Christianity Today,* November 3, 2014, http://www.christianitytoday.com/edstetzer/2014/october/impact-of-migration-on-church.html.

[10] Mark Russell and Daniel Ryumugabe, "Migration, Displacement, and the Kingdom of God," *Lausanne World Pulse* archives, March 2009, http://www.lausanneworldpulse.com/themedarticles-php/1100/03-2009.

This increased fluidity and the psychological adjustments that occur in immigrant communities present an open door for gospel engagement by mission-minded Christians.

Your Muslim neighbor is not someone to be feared. Instead, recognize the upheaval that person has recently experienced in his or her life, recognize the person's fear and lack of cultural awareness, and understand that new neighbors such as yours are willing to listen to you share with them about how you've found hope. If we want to be more evangelistic and see greater numbers of people making commitments to Christ, our Muslim immigrant neighbors may be just the community in which this hope is realized.

We must realize that in an increasingly pluralistic society, with growing numbers of Muslims as our neighbors, local churches are faced with the opportunity to engage their neighbors with the gospel or to eventually die. There are likely no other alternatives.

Dr. Samuel Escobar provides four missiological insights for engaging people who no longer live in their native country:

1. Be compassionate Christians and have loving attitudes, even if this is contrary to popular culture.
2. Equip people to understand contextual issues that Muslim immigrants contend with and to challenge their negative (sinful) attitudes that hinder gospel engagement.
3. Defend those who are weak in your culture, helping them overcome cultural challenges that keep them from being settled and providing for their family.
4. Make migration an avenue for the evangelistic mission.[11]

As Christians, and more specifically as church leaders, we must provide lenses through which our churches view the world. If we desire to see God use his church to engage these transient

---

[11] Samuel Escobar, "Migration: Avenue and Challenge in Mission," *Missiology* 3, no. 1 (January, 2003): 17–28.

communities, we must teach our people how to see the world the way Jesus sees it. We must teach our congregations how to leverage their theology in order to engage in missionary encounters with their neighbors who have a worldview different from their own.

For the entire history of the church, Christians have believed that God is sending us to the nations. At specific times in history, however, God sends the nations to his church. This appears to be one of those moments in history. Let us not miss it. Let us embrace what I believe is a divine and transformative moment, and let us confidently declare and display the gospel of Jesus among our Muslim neighbors for God's glory and for their good.

Reflection Questions

1. How does a personal connection with a Muslim immigrant change the way you view Muslims in general and affect the way the church responds to immigration?
2. What are some practical ways you can serve Muslim immigrants and refugees who have fled violence in their own countries?
3. If you do not already have one or more Muslim friends, how can you go about meeting Muslims who need to hear the gospel?
4. How can you encourage your church to get involved in evangelizing and ministering to Muslim immigrants?
5. What are good strategies for evangelism among Muslim immigrants?

9

Getting to Know Your Muslim Neighbor

D. A. Horton

Evangelism is an issue of the heart. If the heart of the Christian is not burdened for the lost to come to faith in Christ, the privilege and responsibility of sharing the gospel will not be a priority.

In chapter 1, Ed Stetzer introduced the idea of multi-faith engagement to help equip Christians for evangelism to Muslims. The way we approach people who follow another religion impacts our hearts toward them. Stetzer proposed four foundational commitments that Christians can make to help us better engage Muslims with the gospel. He argued that we should: (1) allow followers of a religion to speak for their religion, (2) humanize a religion by talking with individuals who follow the teaching of that faith, (3) respect (even if we don't necessarily agree with) the beliefs of other religions, and (4) honor people with the freedom to determine what they believe.

I want to address the "heart of the matter" when it comes to evangelism. In the North American church, we are seeing a decline in a commitment to personal evangelism. David Kinnaman, president of Barna Group, warns that there is a "growing apathy towards evangelism among the most unlikely of groups: middle-age and middle-income Christians. These are the very people who are often reaching a place of religious maturity, which traditionally includes a commitment to faith-sharing conversations."[1] This Barna study also suggests that millennials are more likely to be evangelistic.

Before we applaud the younger generation too fast, Ed Stetzer challenges this conclusion. A LifeWay Research survey shows that while 85 percent of millennials desire to share the gospel with unbelievers, only 25 percent look for ways to intentionally do so.[2] Further, the survey reveals that among Christians who believe that the only way to heaven is through Jesus Christ, 33 percent of millennials shared their faith in the past six months, compared to 49 percent of those between fifty and sixty-four years of age.

While the studies report different findings, they highlight a common obstacle for Christians of every generation of church history: we face the temptation not to share our faith with the nonbelievers with whom we live in close proximity. This reality, when coupled with the current cultural climate that fosters fear toward Muslims in general—and specifically toward Muslims who are moving into our communities—can increase factors that inhibit personal evangelism. For evangelical Christians, this reality should be unsettling.

A Spiritual Response

In another study, LifeWay Research attempted to untangle why a small percentage of evangelicals who are committed to evangelism do not intentionally share their faith. They found that less than 40 percent of churchgoers have shared their faith with anyone in the

---

[1] "Is Evangelism Going Out of Style?" Barna.com, December 17, 2013. https://www.barna.com/research/is-evangelism-going-out-of-style.

[2] Ed Stetzer, "The State of Evangelism," *Christianity Today*, May 12, 2014, http://www.christianitytoday.com/edstetzer/2014/may/state-of-evangelism.html.

past year, and that almost half of churchgoers have failed to invite an unchurched person to church in the past six months. The study concluded that praying more frequently for the status of those who do not know Christ may be the single-greatest contributing factor to being intentional in sharing one's faith.[3]

In 1 Thess 1:4–10, while expressing a prayer of thankfulness, Paul refers to how the Lord used his example to evangelize the Thessalonians and how the church followed his example in being a faithful evangelistic outpost. In chapter 2, he continues discussing his manner of life among the Thessalonians. He communicates his love and pattern for sharing his life with people as he shares the gospel with them (v. 8).

While Paul is not pointing out blind spots that hinder our evangelistic engagement, as I reflect on what he says about his own evangelistic lifestyle, it seems to me that what is positive about Paul's example hits at three blind spots that contribute to a lack of evangelism. Paul says, "We cared so much for you that we were pleased to share with you not only the gospel of God but also our own lives, because you had become dear to us" (v. 8). The opposite of these patterns of life would hinder effective evangelistic engagement.

- disconnection from one's ministry context
- dichotomized sharing of the gospel and of one's life
- desensitization to the spiritual condition of those around you

Since evangelism is a matter of the heart, Christians will be more prone to share the gospel with unbelievers when they engage their context, share the gospel and their lives with people, and grieve over the spiritual condition of others. While fear and disengagement are temptations for Christians when it comes to Muslims,

[3] Jon Wilke, "Churchgoers Believe in Sharing Their Faith, Most Never Do," LifeWay.com, August 13, 2012, http://www.lifeway.com/Article/research-survey-sharing-christ-2012; no longer accessible.

the goal of this book is to help you develop a love for your Muslim neighbors and to propose a biblical understanding of how you should move forward.

Addressing the Disconnection

Christians must understand that there are at least two types of disconnection between themselves and the lost world around them: a spiritual disconnection and a physical disconnection.

The spiritual divide points to the spiritual difference between those who are Christians and those who are not. Every human being was born a son of the first Adam, and as such, inherited a sin nature from him (Rom 5:12–14). By nature, every person is dead in sin (Eph 2:1–3), a slave to sin (John 8:34), and unable to merit or earn salvation (John 1:11–13; Rom 5:15–21; 1 Cor 1:26–31; Eph 2:8–9; Titus 3:5). The gospel message reminds both believers and unbelievers that it is the finished work of Christ (1 Cor 15:3–4) that wipes our sin debt away, allowing sinners from every ethnicity, gender, and socioeconomic status to be declared not guilty for their sinfulness by God (Rom 4:23–5:1; 5:9; 2 Cor 5:21; 1 Pet 2:24). Embracing the gospel reality leads us to see a division between those who are dead in sin and those who are now alive in Christ (Eph 2:5).

There is also a physical disconnection between believers and unbelievers based on how they live their lives. Believers have been commissioned to remain in the world but not to be of it (John 17:16–19) or to love it (1 John 2:15–17). Therefore, the lifestyle choices of believers do not follow the choices of unbelievers (Eph 5:1–12). In addition, when believers do fall in sin, they are commanded to confess it (1 John 1:8–10); seek spiritual restoration and health from those in the local church (Gal 6:1–2); walk in the assurance of being forgiven by God, knowing they will never face his condemnation or wrath (Rom 8:1); and get back to living on mission.

Because of this physical disconnection, believers can be tempted to build walls of self-preservation. Rather than pressing through awkwardness or personal fear, the majority of believers (regardless of generational labels) privatize their faith, thus remaining disconnected from their community. In 1 Thess 2:8, Paul describes his heart for the Thessalonians and what motivated him to share the gospel with them, saying, "We cared so much for you . . ." In this deeply emotional phrase, Paul expresses an attitude of nurturing, as a mother toward a newborn baby. He also writes in the present tense, meaning that his desire to be with the Thessalonians (as a mother desires to be with her baby) was not a onetime desire but an ongoing one.

Do you want the best for your Muslim neighbors? Do you have a strong desire to be around your unbelieving Muslim friends and neighbors on an ongoing basis? If not, then ask God, who desires for all people to come to salvation (1 Tim 2:1–5; 2 Pet 3:9), to place his desires in your heart so that your desire (Ps 37:4) will be to see unbelievers have an encounter with the gospel that results in faith in Christ. Having a burden to see the lost know Jesus should mobilize believers to engage with unbelievers regardless of life circumstances. It would have been easier for Paul to hide out in Thessalonica rather than engaging in the work of evangelism. Before his coming there, he was treated unjustly in Philippi (Acts 16:11–40; 17:1–9; 1 Thess 2:1–2). In spite of this, he and his fellow workers remained bold with the gospel message.

What is one practical way we can engage our Muslim neighbors in our immediate community? Allow me to share my family's failure to follow through in hopes that it will encourage you not to believe that missed opportunities disqualify you from trying again.

One way my family and I tried to engage our Muslim neighbors was by introducing ourselves to them in a creative way. When we lived in Atlanta, our neighborhood was made up mostly of Hindus and Muslims. Our family wanted to express hospitality, and we thought that baking cookies for the families on on our block would be a good means of introduction. Since we knew that there were dietary restrictions for our Muslim neighbors, we researched which foods were *halāl* (permissible) and which ones were *harām* (prohibited). By doing this, we hoped that our neighbors would see our efforts to respect their convictions, and that this would lead to an open door for future hospitality.

Although we did our research and baked cookies, we failed to take the cookies to our neighbors' homes. We allowed the busyness of life to sidetrack us from reaching out in an initial act of hospitality. By God's grace, we surrendered the grief in our hearts at the missed opportunity and asked the Lord to turn it into a passion to engage our neighbors when we moved to Long Beach, California. To God's glory, he gave us grace to follow through with our new neighbors as we baked and handed out cookies the day after Christmas. Each family in the seven houses we visited were happy and shocked by our gesture. They know our names and we know theirs.

If your neighbors are still outside of a relationship with Christ, each day is an opportunity for you to spend time with them, show them hospitality, and share the gospel.

Addressing the Dichotomy

Relationships are risky. A natural human response is to always keep conversations on a surface level. When engaging with unbelievers, believers face the false dichotomy that says we either share the gospel but not our lives, or share our lives but not the gospel. Believers can overcome this dichotomy by showing off the work of God in their lives, revealing his work of sanctification.

Paul modeled this evangelism practice well as he reminded the Thessalonians that he and his fellow workers were "pleased to share with you not only the gospel of God but also our own lives" (1 Thess 2:8). "We were pleased" expresses Paul's personal, repeated practice of sharing both the gospel and his life with the Thessalonians. The phrase "to share with" means to give part of something away, not the whole of it.[4] It's similar to the young man who donated part of his liver to his little sister. Since the liver is an organ that regenerates, the young man was able to share a piece of his liver, thereby saving his sister's life, and yet still live a full life himself.[5]

But Paul's ministry went even further. Paul shared his *whole self* with the Thessalonians. The substance of his message was the content of the gospel *coupled with* his own life experiences. He did so, not because it was his "official duty," but rather, because he was willing to make himself vulnerable, forming deep relationships so that the people might see God's spiritual work on display in his life. If believers are committed to sharing not only the message of salvation but also the messiness of our sanctification (through a transparent confession of sins), it would promote gospel-saturated conversations, resulting in meaningful missional relationships.

One way I have been able to do this in the marketplace is through casual, on-the job conversations. Whenever coworkers would ask for my opinion on a topic of pop culture, I would explain my point of view from a biblical perspective. The responses have ranged from awkward silence to hostile objections. No matter the initial response, however, I have sought to remain consistent in my beliefs, even in moments of cultural crisis (e.g., 9/11; the Great Recession; the SCOTUS decision of *Obergefell v. Hodges*). Coworkers began to see me struggle alongside them for clarity during such moments. Conversations became more transparent, and I strategically laced more and more Scripture into my responses.

---

[4] Walter Bauer, *A Greek-English Lexicon of the New Testament and Other Early Christian Literature*, ed. William Arndt and Frederick W. Danker (Chicago: University of Chicago Press, 1979), 638.

[5] See Sue Thoms, "Brother Donates Half His Liver to Save Dying Sister in a 'Miracle on the Boulevard,'" MLive Michigan, November 23, 2011, http://www.mlive.com/news/grand-rapids/index.ssf/2011/11/brother_donates_half_his_liver.html.

I'm reminded of two times when such opportunities specifically presented themselves. The first was on September 11, 2001. The community college where I was enrolled was two blocks from the house where I was raised. Although my school was a Catholic institution, nearly half of the student body was Muslim. I recall the tension in the air at school that morning. Many of my Muslim classmates were fearful they would become targets of retaliation; in particular, one young man with whom I had developed a great friendship. We would spend hours standing in the parking lot after class, talking through worldview questions and both of our belief systems.

On this tragic day in America, I sought him out and shared my grief regarding both the events that had taken place and the fear of those students who shared a common faith with him. I shared with him the compassion of Christ and how Jesus's love demonstrated on the cross, in his resurrection from the grave, and in his anticipated return comforts me during times of calamity. I told him that I didn't hold him in contempt for what had taken place, and that I'd like to pray for him if he'd allow me to. Normally he rejected such offers, but this time he accepted. My prayer restated the glorious gospel message coupled with a plea for God's providence to be on my friend's life. I asked that God would do the supernatural work on his heart that only God could do. After I said, "Amen," my friend wiped tears from his eyes, thanked me, and gave me a hug. Little did I know that another believer stood nearby, listening, and was convicted by the way I shared the gospel and the issues of my heart with a person who shared the same faith (broadly speaking) as those reported to have attacked our nation. This believer asked me to pray with him to have a heart of compassion for our Muslim colleagues, and a heart to share not only the gospel but also his life with them by building genuine friendships.

The second opportunity came with the greatest compliment I ever received from an unbelieving coworker. Declaring himself to be an agnostic Buddhist, he told me that if there was ever a person who consistently lived out his beliefs, continuously embraced those who rejected Christianity, and lived in the real world of social angst, it was me. He said that if the gospel I preached was true, then the past two and a half years he had spent with me at work would render him without an excuse before God.

Indeed it was a compliment, but it grieved my heart because I desperately wanted to see him know Jesus. I made one final plea for him to embrace Christ before I left that job. His response matched all his previous responses. He said, "No, thank you," but asked me to pray for him. How could I be desensitized to the condition of his soul after making so many gospel investments in our relationship? The love of God compelled me to continue to pursue missional conversations with him despite all of his rejections of my appeals to place his trust in Christ.

Addressing the Desensitization

If believers are disconnected from the lost around them and do not share their lives and the gospel message with their neighbors, they will likely remain desensitized to their neighbors' spiritual condition. We tend to nonchalantly pass by countless faces in the crowd: dozens of waiters/waitresses who serve us food, Uber drivers that carry us from one destination to another, and neighbors who are only visible when they pull in and out of their garages. Is it possible to carry an equal amount of grief for every person we pass? Probably not. However, believers can be intentional about fighting off desensitization by asking God to give them a grief for the lost who live nearby.

This practice will seem unnatural if believers do not love their neighbors. This sort of love is not the erotic kind, nor even the familial kind, but the sort of love that reflects God's self-sacrificing love. The fuel that drove the apostle Paul's practices toward the Thessalonians was the *agape* love of God. Paul says, "You had become dear to us" (1 Thess 2:8). The Greek word translated as "dear" is *agape*. He declares here that the people have captured his heart. This motivated him to reflect how God loves, both in outward demonstration and in personal relationship.

John 3:16 focuses not on *whom* God loved, but on *how* he loved. God *demonstrated* his love for lost humanity by sending his one unique Son, Jesus, on a mission trip to seek and save the lost. Romans 5:8 defines how Jesus demonstrated his love to sinners—that while *we* were unregenerate, he died in our place on the cross. God's love is experienced in *relationship*. God's steadfast, unconditional love pours out from the pages of Scripture because it is a covenantal book written to the people with whom he is in a covenantal relationship. In Deut 7:9, God expresses his faithfulness to those who love him and keep his commandments. First John 4:7–11 comforts believers with the truth of Jesus as God's covenant-keeping love in person, despite our lack of faithfulness to keep all of his commands. These passages display the constant theme of God's love, demonstrated toward those who share in a covenant relationship with him.

The way we reflect the love of God (1 John 4:7–21) is by distributing it regularly to unbelievers for whom we have a burden, as well as to those in the body of Christ. These two groups encompass the world's population. No person that we encounter should be excluded from receiving a tangible expression of God's love through the way we engage with him or her. If God opens the door for ongoing conversations, and if the *agape* love of God is ruling in our hearts, then we'll be primed to share the gospel with all people.

I've been blessed to have had dozens of conversations with Muslim taxi and Uber drivers in cities across America. If my driver is not on a phone call, I normally ask how his day is going. From there I ask where he is from. This builds a rapport, often leading the driver to ask me why I am in town. Most of the time it is because I'm preaching at a church or speaking at a Christian event. Many times this opens the door for more conversation that can lead to gospel conversations. People want to know how I started preaching. That question allows me to share my conversion story and what life looks like now that I have walked with Jesus for more than twenty years.

Some of my favorite conversations have been with Muslims who shared their personal stories after asking me sincere questions about Jesus and his effect on my life. To date, by God's grace, every Muslim driver I have engaged has granted me permission to pray for him before I get out of the car. Some have even exited the car to shake my hand or give me a hug after thanking me for a great conversation.

I walk away interceding that God, who desires all men to be saved, would send other believers to water the seeds that were just sown, and that God would bring the increase. The *agape* love I have is present in every believer, and this love should lead to a common grief for those who do not know Jesus. This grief should cause us to remain ready to sow and water, all the while walking in freedom, knowing that it is God alone who is responsible for the increase. He alone performs the supernatural work of regeneration. With this in mind, may we be less fearful of sowing and watering.

Conclusion

In order to see more people come to faith in our multiethnic, pluralistic communities, Christians—and specifically evangelicals—must engage in the work of evangelism. We must surrender our hearts to the Lord, asking him to purge us of all forms of selfishness and to prepare us to share our lives with those who live near us. Our hearts will be more prone to share the gospel with saints and sinners when we do these things: engage with our context, share the gospel and our lives with others, and grieve every day over their spiritual condition.

Reflection Questions

1. Would you pray that God would give you a heart for Muslims?
2. What are three tangible ways you can introduce yourself to a Muslim living in or near your community?
3. How might you use your home and your dinner table as opportunities to connect with and befriend your Muslim neighbor?

10

The Challenges Muslims Face in North America

Shirin Taber

Across North America, Islam is often seen as militant, violent, self-righteous, and sectarian. Terrorist attacks and news about growing movements of radical Muslims are frightening. These reports, along with 9/11 and the Iraq and Afghanistan wars, have perpetuated a climate of religious polarization in North America. Both innocent Muslims and Christians have been forced to navigate this challenging situation.

Many Muslims feel their religion has been hijacked. For these Muslims, the rising number of extremists in the West and around the globe who desire ultraconservative interpretations of sharia law, who enforce the veiling of women, and who promote the death penalty for anyone who leaves Islam, marks an uncomfortable shift in their faith and has led to suspicion about Islam from those outside the faith. All of this is creating an identity crisis among Muslims around the world. Some are radicalizing. Some are shamed and frustrated. Some are becoming more secular. Some are leaving the faith. And some are trying to show that Islam can coexist in a multi-faith world.

The media tells the world that 1.2 billion Muslims believe the West is at war with Islam, or vice versa.[1] The climate of war emboldens extremists, giving them a foothold to recruit the next generation (some of whom are now American- and European-born youth). In these communities, Islamic physical violence is promoted. Also, *a terrorism of the soul holds people captive.* Disillusionment, hopelessness, anger, nationalism, distrust, and the quest for wealth and power have led to an increase in Islamic radicalization and religious conflicts. From the powers fueling the Arab Spring, to the Muslim Brotherhood, to the rise of the Islamic State and the Ayatollah's theocracy in Iran, Muslim insurgent groups in the West have grown in recent years.[2]

Many people of Muslim background live peacefully and want the very best for their children and your children. They are navigating a major identity crisis, asking themselves if Islam is a faith they can pass on to their children. They claim, "Islam is best understood not as a set of rigid rules and a list of required rituals but as a story that began with Adam and continues through us; as a tradition of prophets and poets who raised great civilizations by seeking to give expression to the fundamental ethos of faith. . . . The core message of Islam is the establishment of an ethical, egalitarian order on earth."[3] They insist that all the passages of the Quran be read in this light of moral order and merciful justice.

The religious beliefs and practices of Muslims vary depending on many factors, including where they live. Other factors include education, economics, and family dynamics. In the midst of these differences, it is not suprising that many Christians are confused

---

[1] Jahangir E. Arasli, "Violent Converts to Islam: Growing Cluster and Rising Trend," *CTX Journal* 1, no. 1 (August 2011), https://globalecco.org/ctx-v1n1/violent-converts-to-islam.

[2] Arasli.

[3] Eboo Patel, *Acts of Faith: The Story of an American Muslim, in the Struggle for the Soul of a Generation* (Boston: Beacon Press, 2010), 111.

about the true nature of Islam. They know that their Muslim neighbors are peaceful and friendly. But they question the origins and teachings of Islam. They worry about how Islam has evolved in the past thirty years. They question why Muslim-majority nations and communities still restrict women's rights. They question why some Muslims punish or kill other Muslims if their lifestyles, theologies, or religious practices differ. They are horrified by the number of Christians who have been persecuted and killed by some Muslims in the Middle East in the past five years. They fear Muslims who follow an ultraconservative interpretation of sharia in the West; they fear that those Muslims will compromise our democratic society sooner or later. Christians around the world want to know from their political leaders that they will be safe and that Islam will not threaten their way of life.

We are all aware of the terrorist acts at Fort Hood and in Boston, Paris, San Bernardino, Orlando, and Nice. We remember too well the images of the massacre of innocents at the Boston Marathon, the Bataclan theatre, the San Bernardino Christmas party, and the Orlando nightclub. We regularly see images of ISIS, al-Qaeda, and others flying the black flag. Sadly, their violence continues as they fight in the cause of jihad to impose their totalitarian religion on all people.

This climate creates polarization between Christians and Muslims. It also leads to an epidemic of fear toward Muslim people in general. All of this makes it incredibly challenging for Muslims who live in North America.

I speak from experience. As an Iranian American, I have seen firsthand how Muslims are treated in North America. I also speak for the millions of immigrants and refugees fleeing the Middle East, seeking a new home in the West. I am constantly amazed by the growing challenges that Muslims face in my lifetime. The bottom line: Islam is intensifying, and millions of Muslims are suffering a huge identity crisis. The church's response to this must be to join with North American Muslims in resisting extremism and the incursion of dangerous Islamic radicalism.

Even more important, we need to love our enemies as Christ commanded us to do (Matt 22:37–39). We need to explore real pathways for Muslims in North America to thrive and experience the very best that our culture and our nation have to offer. We should also have an honest conversation about (and with) Americans, particularly American Christians, who fear and marginalize North American Muslims. We need to help them understand that our actions can contribute to the problem. Christian anger, prejudice, and avoidance only make next-generation Muslims want to isolate and dig in their heels. Young Muslim people in particular are susceptible to radicalization when they feel like outcasts, unwelcome in our communities. As Christians, we must resist the urge to pull away or attack the growing Muslim immigrant and refugee population. Rather, let us see this unique occurrence in history as a vehicle for the Lord to bring the nations to us.

My purpose in this chapter is to educate Christians on the challenges Muslims face living in North America so we can faithfully pursue loving God and neighbor. Muslims are the fastest-growing religious group in the world. If you don't already have a Muslim neighbor, you will likely have a Muslim living next door to you, working near you, or attending your child's school in the future.

A Little Secret

Let me share a secret with you. When Muslims move to the United States, they expect their neighbors to be Christians. In fact, many Muslims would love to learn about your faith journey. They are curious about church and would love to be invited sometime.

You do not need to debate the merits of Christianity or engage in theological discussions about the Quran and the Bible. Rather, Muslims would be delighted to see you live out and express your faith authentically. Serve with a grateful heart. Give generously of your time, talent, and treasures to causes that help Muslims experience the best that North America and the church have to offer. Take a genuine interest and offer to pray for your Muslim classmate or colleague. Find ways to serve your Muslim neighbors. Include them in your friendship circles at work, at school, and in your neighborhood. Live as a disciple of Christ. You will have an open door to point them to Jesus.

Tear Down through Love

In my book *Muslims Next Door*,[4] I take readers beyond the myth and stereotypes into the real lives of North American Muslims. I tell my story of being the daughter of an immigrant Muslim father during the 1979 hostage crisis in Iran. I also relay the firsthand shame and guilt I felt for being the daughter of a Muslim when America was at odds with the country of my origin. The hostage crisis brought Muslims and the Islamic faith to the forefront of the political debate in our nation. The marginalization I felt (whether self-induced or brought on by my peers) reminds me of the need to keep loving and reaching out to our Muslim neighbors. A person who is "born" a Muslim cannot be judged for the crimes of Muslims thousands of miles away. We must never forget that we cannot judge people who live right next to us for the atrocities that are perpetrated by strangers in foreign lands. My firsthand experience with Muslim conflict and prejudice as a teen reminds me to work toward peacemaking every day going forward.

I am passionate about helping Americans learn how to connect with Muslims in our neighborhoods, workplaces, and college campuses. Efforts to counter violence in Islam and in people connected

---

[4] Shirin Taber, *Muslims Next Door: Uncovering Myths and Creating Friendships* (Grand Rapids: Zondervan, 2004).

to any form of extremism must engage women and men at all levels. With an understanding of the needs of our Muslim neighbors, we can be positive change agents in their families, communities, and public spheres in order to resist the violent "extremisms" that are gripping the world.

Before we can truly love Muslims and share the gospel, we have to deal with the strongholds in our own hearts and minds. We must examine our hearts and tear down the strongholds of fear, anger, bitterness, resentment, suspicion, and especially hatred toward our Muslim neighbors.

Strongholds are areas of land or fortified structures of insurgents—held sometimes for thousands of years—that are able to resist assault and enemy forces. An army that invades enemy territory needs to take down the strongholds to capture the land. If strongholds remain, they will become a continual threat to the citizens in the land.

We have to contend with our strongholds that keep us from loving our neighbors. They emerge from beliefs and emotions, and are birthed and dwell in deception (lies and false beliefs). The best assault against them is the truth of Jesus's teachings. We can expose the lies believed and remind ourselves of what we have in the Healer and Reconciler.

The Scriptures say that our weapons are mighty for the tearing down of strongholds, "since the weapons of our warfare are not of the flesh, but are powerful through God for the demolition of strongholds" (2 Cor 10:4 CSB). Truth dispels deception, and therefore the more truth you bring into a situation, the more the darkness must flee. This is where it is important to apply the words of the New Testament to all areas of our lives: "Perfect love drives out fear" (1 John 4:18). God's Word is our primary weapon for tearing down the strongholds of deception and fear. Our part is to tear down strongholds and to point people to Jesus and to pray for healing and reconciliation.

The best way to move beyond fear is to start with an open and honest conversation. You can take the first step by sharing questions and even anxieties. You can really listen to the thoughts and concerns of another person. Through this process, it is critical to see how one's fear of Muslims creates challenges for North American Muslims and their ability to assimilate in our land. Our fear and ambivalence toward Muslims fuels their insecurity in our communities.

Divisions as big as the divide between Islam and Christianity result in theological, cultural, political, and social points of tensions. Most of those differences we cannot change. However, we can control whether we allow fear to affect how we love another person. If Christians are going to be serious about loving their Muslim neighbor, we need to know that our fear of Muslims reinforces the religious and cultural stereotypes between Muslims and Christians, and does so as we interact with one another personally.

God has given us everything we need to live in peace with our neighbors. Once we deal with the stronghold of fear and repent of it, we then can move on to sharing the gospel with them.

My Personal Journey

Let me end this chapter by sharing a little more about myself. As I previously mentioned, I was raised by an Iranian Muslim father. But my mom is an American Christian. I have lived in the United States, Europe, and the Middle East. With a background in media and cross-cultural training, I assist multiple faith-based initiatives. The *Los Angeles Times, Detroit Free Press,* and Fox News have featured my writing and work among Muslims and Christians alike. Previously I served with Cru, the *Jesus Film* Project, and the Christian Broadcasting Network. I am a graduate of the University of Washington and fluent in English, French, and Farsi.

Today my work is a like a two-sided coin. On one hand, I advocate and lecture for peacemaking toward Muslims. I speak at churches, Christian colleges, and organizations about building trust with our Muslim neighbors. On the other hand, I support the efforts of the persecuted church in the Middle East, which has suffered greatly during the rise of Islamic radicalism.

As a director of the Middle East Women's Leadership Network, I equip women to become world-class leaders by creating media for their mission. We equip television producers, filmmakers, writers, artists, activists, and ministry leaders.[5] Having served in the Middle East, I know firsthand the powerful influence of discipleship, mentoring, and authentically coming alongside the next generation. Over the past twenty years, I have seen countless lives changed by the gospel through intentional relational investments. Many women are now living fruitful lives as wives, mothers, employees, and agents of change.

I regularly speak on the vital role that Westerners play in helping next-generation Muslims assimilate and pursue personal freedoms. For millions of people around the world, Westerners represent innovation, freedom of expression, women's rights, and the pursuit of happiness. We inspire people to think outside the box, listen to their dreams, and lean into their challenges.

In the Middle East in particular, core changes are needed if all people (women, youth, disabled, minorities, the poor) are to be treated with equality and full recognition of their giftedness. All the more, the next generation of Muslims needs role models who can support and guide them. With the desire to empower emerging leaders, we must continue to focus on their need to strengthen relationships, receive training, develop practical plans, and partner in collaborative initiatives to strengthen our societies.

In 2015, I was asked by the GWB Women's Leadership Initiative to mentor Eli, a Tunisian female and Islamic studies professor. Eli is extremely gifted in her field. Eli and I worked together to expand her

[5] See www.mideastwomen.org for more information.

leadership platform through media, lecturing, networking, and hosting a peace summit. Additionally, I developed a better understanding of the challenges Muslims face and the forces that grow terrorism in the West. While Eli visited me in California, we embarked on several fascinating counter-radicalism interviews that I set up through my relational networks. We discussed ways that media and women's networks can share a counter-radicalism narrative.

I was first introduced to terrorism as a nine-year-old girl living in Iran. My father worked for Iran Airlines. I remember coming home from school one day and my mother telling me that my American neighbor, a high-ranking military official, had been assassinated on his way to work.

When I was in my twenties, I lived in Paris, and I heard about the bombings on the metro related to the nearby war in Algeria. Several of the students I served as a university chaplain fled Algeria because of the great violence there.

Then I learned about increasing acts of terror in the United States. I was in Tunis with a group of American students during the Columbine shootings. The shootings horrified me, especially since I had lived in Denver for three years before moving to France. Afterward, we experienced 9/11, the Fort Hood shootings, the Boston Massacre, and other tragic incidents.

It was the Paris attacks, however, that deeply impacted me and helped me truly align myself with Eli's work. My eighteen-year-old daughter was studying abroad in Paris, and suddenly she was caught in the middle of the Paris massacre. She was just three blocks from the concert hall where eighty people were gunned down. I remember texting her during a lockdown situation. I felt angry that my child was in harm's way in the middle of this act of terror. But then I remembered my work with Eli and realized this is now my calling too.

A wave of calm came over me. Although my daughter's life is now marked by terrorism, I know that Eli and I are working together to stop cultural and religious-based violence. We now both commit to mobilizing women of peace. Today, Eli continues her work by speaking to the media and at global-level events. She also has made significant progress in sharing with Tunisian parliament members and the president's cabinet.

Who is your Eli? What Great Commission opportunities has the Lord given you to engage Muslims with the gospel? Perhaps it will start in a way that my relationship with Eli started—we worked together for a common purpose. Is the Lord calling you to come alongside Muslims in North America to help them or to address a common need in your community? How can you help Muslims overcome the challenges they face living in North America? Do you know someone you can invest in?

The starting place for these types of opportunities is prayer. If you don't know someone you can engage, pray that the Lord will bring someone into your life. Look for someone in your community. A parent of one of your kid's classmates. A local business owner. A student who has come to your community to attend college. You should then pray that the Lord will give you a compassionate love toward that person. Pray for the Lord to give you opportunities to talk with and serve him or her, and to build a meaningful relationship.

Conclusion

Yes, some aspects within Islam are intensifying. Things may get much more challenging in the years to come. But we are more than overcomers through Christ. As disciples of Jesus, we will be known by our love. In fact, we are commanded to love our enemies; at the least, it requires relating to them and engaging them with our lives. As we said previously, your Muslim neighbors will not be surprised that you are a Christian. They will expect it, and they will more than likely be open to talking to you about what you believe.

At the beginning of this book, Ed Stetzer suggested four foundational commitments that Christians should make as they engage people of other faiths:

1. Let each religion speak for itself.
2. Talk with and about *individuals,* not generic "faiths."
3. Respect others who hold to different beliefs, just as you would expect them to respect you for yours.
4. Grant each person the freedom to make his or her faith decisions.

These principles provide simple guidelines to help you engage in Great Commission opportunities. They will help you resist anxiety and fear over not knowing what to say and feeling the pressure that you have to know everything about Islam. Stetzer's principles rightly warn us that our prior knowledge should not get in the way of actually listening to people's beliefs and ideas. We are called to engage real people with the life-transforming message of the gospel.

Most of all, I believe that these principles, if put into application, will help you serve Muslims in your community and assist them in overcoming some of the challenges they face in living in North America. By doing this, you can take Great Commission opportunities and turn them into gospel conversations.

At the end of this chapter, I return to a question that I asked earlier: Who is your Eli? Whether you know who that individual is right now, I leave you with this final exhortation: pray for that person.

Reflection Questions

1. What preconceived notions do you have about Muslims, and are they negatively affecting your ministry to Muslims (or causing you to avoid such ministry altogether)?

2. Would you feel comfortable inviting a Muslim friend to your church? Why or why not?
3. What are ways you can partner with Muslims to work against injustice in the world? How does this create gospel opportunities with Muslims?

11

Muslims and the Great Commission: The Importance of Community

Ant Greenham

Arabs love proverbs. One of my favorites goes something like this: *Your family can save you from anything—but nothing can save you from your family!* It is meant to be funny, but it illustrates a deep truth, not only in the Arab world, but in Muslim societies generally. The point is that Muslims are typically born into, grow up in, and are embraced their entire lives by community. That community is their security; but as we shall see, it is also their prison. Including their immediate and wider family, their community extends to the entire body of Muslims across the globe.

This Muslim community is typically called the *ummah*. As Reza Aslan explains, from the beginning of Islam, the *ummah* provided "a common social and religious identity that allowed one group to distinguish itself from another." Moreover, "unlike a traditional tribe, [it] had an almost unlimited capacity for growth through conversion."[1]

[1] Reza Aslan, *No God but God: The Origins, Evolution and Future of Islam*, 2nd ed. (New York: Random House, 2011), 58.

In other words, Muslims derive a key part of their identity from membership in a (growing) worldwide religious community.

Ummah: The Challenges of Muslim Evangelism

The concept of *ummah*, religious communal identity, has key implications for anyone wanting to see Muslims become disciples of the Lord Jesus Christ (and that applies to everyone seeking to fulfill the Great Commission). For apart from the need to persuade a Muslim of the truth of Jesus's person and message, which is integral to becoming his disciple, one must consider the reaction of that person's community. Muslims claim to respect Jesus (or *Isa*, as they call him), but only as a great, and now surpassed, prophet. Critically, as a group, the Muslim *ummah* rejects the very heart of the gospel: the death and resurrection of Jesus, the Son of God. And this rejection intensifies when it comes to baptism.

For Christians, water baptism publicly demonstrates one's embrace of Christ as Lord and Savior and is inherent to obeying the Great Commission.[2] In contrast, the Quran's Surah 2:138 reads, "[Our religion] takes its hue from Allah and who can give a better hue than Allah. It is He. Whom we worship."[3] At first glance, this has nothing to do with baptism, Christian or otherwise. However, as Kenneth Cragg argues, the phrase translated "hue from Allah" is best understood as "the baptism of God."[4] Islam, then, is the baptism of Allah.

---

[2] Cf. Matt 28:19–20.

[3] *The Holy Quran: Text, Translation and Commentary*, trans. Abdulah Yusuf Ali (Elmhurst, NY: Tahrike Tarsile Qur'an, 2001).

[4] Kenneth Cragg, *Jesus and the Muslim: An Exploration* (London: George Allen & Unwin, 1985; repr., Oxford: Oneworld, 1999), 234.

As Harry K. Wilson III notes, "What Christian baptism had not done ... the Islamic baptism is said to do."[5] Muslims are the recipients of this "baptism" simply by being Muslim (as part of the *Ummah*). At the center of all of this is a sense of community cohesiveness that should not be broken for any reason. Wilson suggests "that the Islamic collective consciousness, *nahniyah* ['we-ness'], is one of the main sources if not the main source, of the stigma of baptism in Islamic culture. . . . [Christian] baptism represents a public breakdown in the 'we.' . . . What was tantamount to suicide in tribal Arabia, the forsaking of the tribe, has been transferred to the forsaking of the Islamic *dar* (house)."[6] Consequently, a Muslim who converts to Jesus and is baptized "is cast outside of the Islamic 'we,' into the Christian 'they.'"[7] Muslim converts to Christ are thus understandably cautious about associating visibly with Christian congregations (or admitting they have been baptized).

Sufyan Baig, a Christian who grew up as a practicing Muslim, explains the dilemma as follows: A Muslim's "life within the *ummah* has been a place of security, acceptance, protection, and identity. For a seeker, it is an enormous sacrifice to lose his place in the *ummah*."[8] Baig goes on to explain his own experience of being purged from the *ummah*. After his conversion, his father gave him

> six months to decide whether to follow this new faith or to remain in the *ummah* and enjoy all the pleasures of wealth and family. When I chose the Christian faith, my father asked me to walk out of my home with only the clothes I

---

[5] Harry K. Wilson III, *The Stigma of Baptism in the Evangelization of Muslims: An Historical and Critical Evaluation* (Fort Worth: Southwestern Baptist Theological Seminary, 1995), 20.

[6] Wilson, 42.

[7] Wilson, 78.

[8] Sufyan Baig, "The *Ummah* and Christian Community," in David Greenlee, ed., *Longing for Community: Church, Ummah, or Somewhere in Between?* (Pasadena, CA: William Carey Library, 2013), 71.

> was wearing. . . . One day I was living as a wealthy businessman; the next day, for the sake of food and shelter, I was cleaning toilets in an orphanage for street children.[9]

Baig relates the experiences of others' expulsion from the *ummah* too, including the sad case of Yusuf Wahid. Threatened with death if he did not return, and lacking "concrete support from his Christian community—Yusuf returned to the *ummah*."[10] Sadly, this is not an uncommon outcome, primarily because of the Islamic law against apostasy.

Practically, this long-standing law has meant that an apostate (i.e., one who leaves the faith of Islam) is subject to the death penalty. Although the Quran does not explicitly state that an apostate should be executed, a number of *ahadith* (traditions of the words and actions of Muhammad) make it clear that he commanded the death of apostates.[11] As a result, the death penalty for apostasy has been part of Islamic law (sharia) from the earliest times. Religious tolerance is sometimes argued on the basis of Surah 2:256, which states there should be no compulsion in religion, but in Islamic jurisprudence, this is never applied to apostates.

As Bernard Lewis explains, tolerance may not "be extended to the apostate, the renegade Muslim, whose punishment is death. Some authorities allow the remission of this punishment if the apostate recants [e.g., Yusuf Wahid]. Others insist on the death penalty even then. God may pardon him in the world to come; the law must punish him in this world."[12]

It may be granted that all of this applies differently from one place to the next. Muslims in the West typically do not face anything resembling the law against apostasy on local statute books. But they

---

[9] Baig, 72.

[10] Baig, 73.

[11] Al Bukhari 4.52.260, 9.84.58, 9.84.64.

[12] Bernard Lewis, *The Middle East: A Brief History of the Last 2,000 Years* (New York: Touchstone, 1995), 230.

are part of the *ummah*, with all its constraints, including centuries of precedence that apostates be executed.

Muslims Do Come to Christ

It is thus apparent that considerable barriers, tied together by community cohesiveness, inhibit those seeking to make disciples of Muslims. Nevertheless, Muslims do come to Christ!

With my wife's assistance, I interviewed a number of Palestinian Muslim converts to Christ in January 2003 for my PhD dissertation.[13] We found that the individuals concerned were influenced by a number of different conversion factors, but the overall picture for the group had the person of Jesus at the center. The converts were drawn to him through various means. These were God's miraculous involvement, the truth of his message, believers' roles, Bible reading, and an array of other factors. Nevertheless, Jesus was always central. In contrast, very few were converted because they rejected Islam. These patterns were supported by findings drawn from literature on Muslim conversions, assessments of missionaries who worked with Palestinians, and results from a control group of ten male converts interviewed in Bangladesh.

Applying these findings, it would seem that a divine/human synergy is involved as one seeks to make disciples of Muslims. Converts encounter the person of Jesus by the power of God. He must act for conversion to occur. However, believers have a crucial role to play in pointing Muslims to Jesus. Quite simply, they do so by presenting the biblical truth about him. Where literacy is a problem, the Bible's testimony to Jesus may be presented via other means. This

[13] Ant Greenham, *Muslim Conversions to Christ: An Investigation of Palestinian Converts Living in the Holy Land*, Evangelical Missiological Society Dissertation Series, ed. Richard L. Starcher (Pasadena, CA: WCIU Press, 2004).

communicative process will probably be lengthy, but believers' consistency and sincerity are essential.

At the same time, those who convert are only transformed as they sincerely turn to Jesus. In sum, missionaries must do their part, but the Lord coordinates the details. So, one should never move from dependence on him.

Rejection and Acceptance: A Call for Christian Community

Moving beyond these key conversion factors and the imperative that we trust the Lord throughout the process, one must recall the role of community in a Muslim's life. Typically, Muslims do not set out to reject their faith,[14] let alone the *ummah,* should they consider the person of Christ. In fact, consideration of Jesus aside, it is probable that Muslims in North America tend to rely *more* on the familial security provided by the *ummah* in our intensely individualistic culture, than they would in communal Muslim societies.

Earlier this year, I received a prayer request that points to this very challenge: "Missionaries who have lived among the Wolof [a West African people group] have found it difficult to evangelize them. One reason is that it is hard for them to leave the community and be self-reliant."[15] This challenge is easy to explain. If your life and identity have been defined and supported by a group of people around you, people who have helped you navigate the challenges of a particular culture, then separating from that community presents

---

[14] This may be changing in some cases as Muslims are repelled by atrocities performed by ISIS and other groups in their name. However, a Muslim who rejects his or her religion is not automatically a new disciple of Jesus Christ. There is a phenomenon of Muslims rejecting their faith for agnosticism or atheism (while remaining nominally Muslim in some cases). But that is not the outcome we seek as Great Commission Christians!

[15] Protected source.

a scary new world that isolates you from those who once provided security and support and in whom you once found meaning and significance. The risk of the new world is felt even more when one forsakes his or her community or is forsaken by them with no new community with whom to identify.

Unfortunately, while a new believer may have no intention of abandoning his or her secure social network, rejection (or worse) by the *ummah* is a common phenomenon, as we have seen. This is no exception in America. Hass Hirji-Walji was a young refugee from Idi Amin's Uganda who moved to Minnesota with his family. As a Muslim in his new homeland, he had no time for the licentious lifestyles of many fellow students. He felt more comfortable with evangelical Christians, but hoped to convert them to Islam.[16] These relationships led him to ask many questions about Christianity, and he discovered that the God of the Bible seeks humanity, not the other way around. He was also struck by his Christian contacts' assurance of forgiveness. After struggling with fears of losing his family and Muslim identity, he implored God to show him the way. With great difficulty, but with an enabling he did not understand, he had a believer lead him in a prayer of surrender to Christ. He resisted a later temptation to return to Islam, experienced family rejection, and was assaulted by Muslim thugs in Minneapolis. However, he was kept secure by the promise that Christ would never abandon him (Heb 13:5).[17]

A key issue here, as always, is the Lord's care of his sheep (see John 10:27–29). Personal repudiation was nevertheless part of Hirji-Walji's experience, and this is where fellow believers have a role to play. In a nutshell, a new disciple from a Muslim background must feel that joining a Christian fellowship is far more valuable than leaving the *ummah*.

---

[16] Hass Hirji-Walji and Jaryl Strong, *Escape from Islam* (Wheaton, IL: Tyndale, 1981), 69.

[17] Hirji-Walji and Strong, 110.

What does this mean? A Christian's friendly words about the new believer's wonderful conversion story, a promise to pray for that person, and a stated intention to see him or her at church next week aren't enough. Apart from the fact that such undertakings are frequently unfulfilled, belonging requires far more than a brief interchange and prayer, followed (perhaps) by more of the same somewhere in the future. In sum, the fallback "self-reliance" of American culture simply doesn't satisfy a Muslim who is grasping for community with his or her new Christian family.

Interestingly, David Brickner of Jews for Jesus, who operates in the same individualistic church context but as a Jewish believer, has similar insights:

> Often the body of Messiah (also known as the church) is undervalued. Perhaps that's because of our overly developed sense of individualism, especially in Western culture. As believers in Jesus are discipled into the faith, personal redemption tends to be the central focus. Yet the Scripture—and Jesus' entire life and ministry—clearly reveal that God's plan was not just to save individual souls, but also to establish this new and mysterious family.[18]

The challenge, then, is twofold: How do we build this (mysterious) family, and especially, how do we include new disciples from a Muslim background who particularly long for it?

The bottom line, quite simply, is that we must do community well ourselves if we are to offer something meaningful to folks expelled from the *ummah*. Perhaps Jesus's words of encouragement to his disciples as he commissioned them to make disciples, are a good place to start: "I am with you always, to the end of the age"

---

[18] David Brickner, "Our Mysterious Family," *Jews for Jesus Newsletter* 5776, no. 11 (July 2016), http://jewsforjesus.org/publications/newsletter/jul-2016/our-mysterious-family.

(Matt 28:20). What might be missed here is the plural "you." He is with *us*, not just with me. This continues Jesus's disciple-making strategy, where he spent time with his disciples in smaller and larger groups, often (though not always) in someone's home.[19] Since this is the case, we should make disciples (and so fulfill the Great Commission) in the same way.

We must commit to being with and understanding fellow believers. In other words, what I like to call "biblical friendship" is required. This is difficult to grasp, because (biblical) friendship is so easily confused with friendliness. A smiling, friendly face and the interchange of a few lighthearted, even sincere, comments are certainly pleasant enough, but that's not the same as true friendship. I think the problem here is our use of the word "friend." Colleagues and neighbors call each other friends no matter how superficial the relationship. Politicians love to address potential supporters with the title "friend." A favorite bakery of ours has a sign telling anyone at the door: "Arrive as a Customer, Leave as a Friend." And the phenomenon is enhanced by the explosion of "friends," people you hardly know, on Facebook. In that sense, just about anyone can be your friend.

To illustrate this shallow understanding of friendship, a student of mine recently told the class that he had been abroad, met a local he liked, and then introduced him to someone else as his "friend." To his surprise, his new acquaintance immediately corrected him with the words, "I'm not your friend!" What the acquaintance meant, it seems, is that being someone's friend goes way beyond initial friendliness. There has to be a commitment, proven over time.

---

[19] The homes were sometimes those of unbelievers, but the disciples certainly learned valuable lessons in such settings, as the record of what transpired in each case would attest. Examples of home environments from the third Gospel include Luke 5:29; 7:36; 10:38; 11:37; 14:1; 19:7; 22:7–14; 24:30.

Building Biblical Friendships

So how do we do Great Commission (i.e., biblical) friendship, the key to building our new family in the Lord? Using Jesus as our example, it's interesting that he told his disciples they were his confidants, not his servants, and as such, his friends (John 15:15). As his friends, he would love them by laying down his life for them, but they were to love each other the same way (John 15:12–14). In other words, Great Commission friendship (i.e., truly making disciples) means being a vulnerable, understanding, sacrificial friend, like Jesus, to others. Not only that, it has to be for the long haul.

Ultimately, this enduring demand is always higher than anything we can attain. But we can take a stab at it in the following ways:

1. *Focus on a few.* Jesus did. His closest relationships were with just three disciples. I think this is a good guideline; you can't have deep friendships with everybody.
2. *Be deliberate in establishing friendships.* My wife and I did this with another couple. It started with a few shared meals—in our homes—involving an in-depth sharing of values and ideas right before they took a trip to the Middle East. But we agreed that we shouldn't throw the relationship away once they returned and their trip was no longer the focus. As fellow believers growing in the Lord, there were numerous things to share! And so, eight years later, we are still spending quality time with each other, pretty much on a monthly basis.
3. *Be on the lookout—and pray for—folks to befriend.* Given the subject of this chapter, that should certainly include Muslims who've been forced out of the *ummah*. However, the Lord may have specifics for you that don't fit a neat, predetermined pattern. Whatever you do, send a clear message that the friendship you offer enhances long-term belonging, whether the folks concerned are believers or not in the beginning.

4. *Finally, show respect.* In particular, don't violate your friends' freedom. It is all too easy to adopt a "we know better" (or worse, "we have the money") attitude, and insist on giving folks things they neither want nor need. Listen to and learn from your friends, allowing them an equal voice as the relationship unfolds.

It might be helpful to conclude on an academic yet practical note. Alan Totire conducted his PhD research on factors facilitating a positive Christian identity (which enhanced a sense of belonging) among groups of Muslim-background believers (MBBs) in North America, and has the following observation: "Since Muslims generally come from relational cultures, it is important to form a small group of people in the church who are willing to be a part of their community. Optimally, it should include a leader who understands cultures well, such as a missionary or ethnic pastor." He goes on to argue that MBBs be allowed "opportunities to make friendships with Christians from other backgrounds. [Totire] . . . found many of [his] participants excited to be part of a new family in Jesus Christ. They see the Gospel as inclusive of all, and would want to meet others within that family."[20] What this means is that Christians should encourage the formation of small groups, open to others, that Muslim-background believers can join, but led by a culturally sensitive individual.

I would emphasize, in closing, that such groups must meet in *homes*. I say this because homes typically provide a sense of security and intimacy lacking in other contexts. This will engender the new-family belonging that former members of the *ummah* crave. All this

[20] Alan Totire, "Attaining a Positive Christian Identity (Part 2): Retention and Discipleship in Local Churches," COMMA (A Coalition of Ministries to Muslims in North America), September 1, 2015, http://commanetwork.com/dig_deeper/attaining-a-positive-christian-identity-part-2-retention-and-discipleship-in-local-churches.

takes planning and effort, of course. But if we are serious about fulfilling the Great Commission, I do not believe there is any other way.

Reflection Questions

1. What can you learn from Muslims and how they do community?
2. Are you involved in a community to which you could invite a Muslim?
3. At present, do you do community well? Why does this matter when it comes to evangelizing Muslims? What can you do better?
4. Is it difficult for you to empathize with Muslims who are very communal in nature? Why or why not?
5. Are you willing to make sacrifices to disciple a new believer converting out of Islam? What might some of those sacrifices be?

12

Sharing the Gospel with a Muslim

Afshin Ziafat

I grew up in an Iranian Muslim home. I was born in Houston, and my family moved back to Iran when I was two. The Islamic Revolution of Iran precipitated my family's return to Houston when I was six. When I was seven, I received a New Testament from my second-grade tutor, and ten years later, by reading that New Testament, I came to faith in Christ.

As a Muslim-background believer in Christ, I am passionate about our call to engage Muslims with the gospel. Before we spend time discussing how to share our faith with Muslims, I want to spend some time laying out some of the beliefs and ideologies of Islam so that we have a better understanding of where they are coming from. I want to focus on their view of God, man, Jesus, and salvation, and how those beliefs motivate their lives.

View of God

The foundational teaching of Islam is that God is one. Most Muslims believe Islam to be the only true monotheistic religion. They do not understand the Christian concept of the Trinity. They believe Christians worship three Gods: Father, Son, and Holy Spirit. They do not understand that the Bible teaches one God who has expressed and revealed himself to us in three persons. The Muslim God, Allah, is seen as being wholly other, transcendent over his universe and over his creation. Muslims can know about God (there are ninety-nine beautiful names of Allah), but there is not an intimate, personal relationship with God as Christians experience in Christ. In fact, the word *Islam* means "submission to Allah," and the word *Muslim* means "one who submits to Allah."

Islam is primarily a religion about submitting to Allah, his rules, and his commands. Although submission to God's commands is an outworking of the Christian faith, Christianity views God not as a taskmaster but as a Father. Jesus taught his disciples to pray, "Abba, Father" (see Matt 6:9). John calls us to behold the love of God seen in the fact that we should be called "God's children" (1 John 3:1). So, in Christianity, there is a relationship with God as Father, and the result is not just submission but conformity to Christ.

View of Man

In Islam, man is believed to be born sinless. In Christianity, it is exactly the opposite. The Bible teaches that all humankind is born in sin. In fact, David declared, "I was sinful when my mother conceived me" (Ps 51:5). David took sin not just to birth but all the way back to conception. If you believe that you are born sinless, then there is nothing to be saved from. Therefore, it is important to note that the idea of a need for a Savior is foreign to most Muslims.

I once heard a Muslim scholar say, "I liken the notion of Jesus to my sitting on a dock and a man running by, throwing himself in the water, and drowning himself to prove his love to me. It's absurd." And here you see the key difference. A Muslim thinks he is on a dock; he thinks he is fine. But a Christian understands that he is in the water, drowning and in need of a Savior; or better yet, a Christian understands that he is under the water, dead. As Paul says in Eph 2:1, "You were dead in your trespasses." Because we are in that condition, we must be made alive in Christ. Islam and Christianity approach the state of man from a totally different starting point.

View of Jesus

Muslims believe that Jesus was a prophet in a line of prophets that include Adam, Noah, Abraham, Moses, and Muhammad, who was the completer of their faith. Jesus was merely a good human prophet. He was not one with God.

The greatest sin in Islam is the sin of *shirk*, which is to equate anything or anyone with God. So, for Muslims to wrap their minds around the idea of Jesus being God in human form is a huge hurdle. However, Muslims believe two things about Jesus that are consistent with our view of Christ's deity. They believe that he was born of a virgin, and they believe that he lived a sinless life. Muslims acknowledge that Jesus is like no other human who has walked the earth. Christians understand that these truths about Jesus reveal that he is God. The prophet Isaiah said that a virgin shall give birth to a son, and his name shall be Immanuel (Isa 7:14). The word "Immanuel" means "God with us," not "Prophet with us." Additionally, the Bible says that there is no human who is righteous, not even one, and that only God is sinless (Rom 3:10).

What do Muslims believe about the death of Jesus? They do not believe that he was crucified. In fact, the Quran says that it only appeared that he was crucified. Many Muslim commentators interpret this by saying that God performed a miracle by making Judas look like Jesus and that the wrong man was crucified. There are many problems with this theory. The first problem is that the Bible teaches that Jesus in fact died; and next, the Bible teaches that Judas hung himself. Ultimately, Muslims do not have a good explanation for the historical account of Jesus's crucifixion except to say that it merely appeared to happen. The implication of their denial of the cross is that they have a totally different view of mankind's means of salvation.

View of Salvation

Islam teaches that there will be a day of judgment. At the judgment day, Muslims will face a scale that weighs all their good deeds against their bad deeds. Whether they will enter eternal paradise will be determined by if their good deeds outweigh their bad deeds. I have spoken to many Muslims who are quick to point out that Allah is a forgiving God, but there is no accounting for the basis of Allah's forgiveness. Thus, there is no way around the fact that Islam teaches that man must earn God's favor.

Many Christians also mistakenly believe that the Bible teaches that we have to earn salvation by doing good deeds. The Bible does not teach that you earn your salvation by being 51 percent good. It teaches that if you want to be judged on the basis of your deeds, you must be 100 percent good to merit your eternal reward. God is sinless, holy, and perfectly righteous. His standard is 100 percent perfection. The Bible teaches in Rom 3:23, "All have sinned and fall short of the glory of God." For this reason, for Christians, Jesus Christ is our only hope for salvation. He lived a sinless life so that he would shed his perfect blood on the cross to pay for our sins. If we receive Christ and his work on the cross through faith, then when we die, God is not going to weigh our good and bad deeds on a scale.

He's going to look at our lives and see Christ's blood covering us. He is going to receive us because of what Jesus has done.

Islam is essentially a religion of works, and Christianity is a message of grace. Many Muslims think that the Christian doctrine of salvation by grace alone through faith in Christ alone is absurd, because if salvation is a free gift, there is no motivation for living for God. The Bible is clear that grace does not lead to a freedom to sin, but rather, to a freedom to truly live for God (Rom 6:15–18).

A true Christian will produce good works, but his good works are not a means to his salvation. Rather, they are a product of his salvation, or better put, a proof of his salvation. Scripture teaches in James, "Faith without works is dead" (2:26). Why does a Christian live for God? Christians live for God not out of fear of going to hell, because the Christian understands that his place in heaven is already secured by the blood of Christ. A Christian lives for God ultimately because of love. Paul says it this way: "For the love of Christ compels us, since we have reached this conclusion: If one died for all, then all died. And he died for all so that those who live should no longer live for themselves, but for the one who died for them and was raised" (2 Cor 5:14–15 CSB). So we live for Jesus, not because he is holding hell over our heads, but because he has removed the wrath of God by his blood and given us favor with God. Because he first loved me, I live for him (1 John 4:19).

Christians believe that God is more honored when we live for him in response to his love for us than out of fear. Love is the greatest motivator. Love will cause you to lay your life down and live for God, just as he laid his life down for you. Love is the central idea that we need to keep in mind as we engage with Muslims. The unconditional love of God is what Muslims most need to see and hear from us. Listen to how the apostle John said it in his first epistle:

> And we have come to know and to believe the love that God has for us. God is love, and the one who remains in love remains in God, and God remains in him. In this, love is

> made complete with us so that we may have confidence in the day of judgment, because as he is, so also are we in this world. There is no fear in love; instead, perfect love drives out fear, because fear involves punishment. So the one who fears is not complete in love. We love because he first loved us. (1 John 4:16–19 CSB)

This is how we engage Muslims with the gospel—by loving them. Loving them enough to pray for them, welcome them, serve them, and share with them.

After I became a Christian, I learned that there was a group of high school seniors who had committed to pray for over a year for my salvation. I believe that prayer is the beginning of evangelism. In Luke 10, when Jesus sent out the seventy-two disciples into every place that he was about to go, he asked them to first pray that the Lord would send more laborers. I love that the first command of the Lord in this mission was to pray. Paul commanded Timothy to instruct the church to pray for all because God desires all men to be saved and to come to a knowledge of the truth (1 Tim 2:1–4). I have met many Muslims who have come to faith in Christ through a vision or a dream, simply because a missionary or converted family member was praying for them. When we pray for Muslims, not only does God work on their hearts; he works on our hearts. We begin to see Muslims the way God sees them—with compassion and love. One of the best things we can do is to ask Muslims how we can pray for them.

Matthew 28 calls Christians to make disciples of all nations, and Acts 1:8 says that we are to be witnesses of Christ to the ends of the earth. In our day, the "ends of the earth" are moving into our neighborhoods here in North America. Muslims are immigrating to our cities in record numbers. Most of us do not need to board a plane to take the gospel to the Muslim world; we only need to cross the street to our neighbor's house.

Many of our Muslim neighbors are new to our culture and need help assimilating. One of the best ways to see the hearts of Muslims open up to hearing about the salvation that is offered to them based on Jesus's death, burial, and resurrection is to remember how God treated us when we were outsiders. Then, we are to do likewise in loving the foreigner and sojourner among us. Moses wrote, "You will regard the alien who resides with you as the native-born among you. You are to love him as yourself, for you were aliens in the land of Egypt; I am the Lord your God" (Lev 19:34 CSB). The gospel reminds us that we were once not part of God's people, but by God's mercy are now made part of his people (1 Pet 2:10).

Unfortunately, because of the rise of radical Islamic terrorism, many have made the mistake of becoming suspicious of all Muslims. The recent Syrian refugee crisis brought this fear to the forefront. We need to ask ourselves how we should respond if a Muslim moves into our neighborhood. Putting aside the fact that it is highly unlikely that a Muslim neighbor seeks my harm, Christian safety ought not be our primary concern. We are to be driven by our mission to be the hands and feet of Christ and to be his ambassadors, sharing the gospel with all nations.

In the story of the good Samaritan, could it be that the priest and the Levite passed by the man who was beaten and in need of assistance because they feared their own safety? After all, what if the same fate were to befall them? The good Samaritan, however, stepped into the situation and sacrificially took care of the man. We are to do likewise. In his speech to the Ephesian elders in Acts 20, Paul stated that he knew suffering awaited him in Jerusalem, but almost as if he anticipated someone dissuading him from going to Jerusalem, he stated that his life wasn't even the most valuable thing to him, but rather, his mission to spread the gospel (v. 24). We love Muslims by inviting them into our homes for dinner, asking how we can help them assimilate into our community—helping set up bank accounts, helping sign up their kids for school, whatever it may be.

As we get to know our Muslim neighbor, classmate, or coworker and learn of his or her needs, we seek to meet those needs. Paul wrote, "Although I am free from all and not anyone's slave, I have made myself a slave to everyone, in order to win more people" (1 Cor 9:19 CSB). If we want to share the gospel with a Muslim, we must often first earn the right to be heard by the way we serve him. Before a Muslim cares to know what you believe, he must know that you care, especially when he may expect to be ostracized.

As I mentioned, my family moved back to the United States when I was six because of the unrest in Iran due to the revolution. We had no idea what we would face in America. Shortly after coming to this country, the Iranian hostage crisis hit. A group of Americans were held hostage in Iran, and it was not easy for us to live in Houston. Many people persecuted us because they knew my family was from Iran. I am so thankful for one Christian lady who did not see my family as a threat but as an opportunity to advance the gospel. My Christian tutor loved me and met a real need in my life by teaching me the English language. She did this during a time when others threw bricks through the windows of our home or threatened to beat up my brother and me. Had any other American given me the New Testament, I would've thrown it away because I didn't trust many Americans in that day. But I'm thankful it came from the one who was showing me the love of Christ in her actions. Since it came from her, I held on to that New Testament, and I would read it years later and come to faith in Christ.

As we pray for Muslims, get to know them, welcome them, and serve them, doors will be opened to have conversations with them about the most important thing in life. A significant element of our sharing Jesus with Muslims comes first through asking questions and listening to them. In Acts 8, when Philip starts a gospel conversation with an Ethiopian sitting in a chariot, reading from the book of Isaiah, Philip begins by asking a question: "Do you understand what you're reading?" (Acts 8:30). Now, we may never find a Muslim reading from the Old Testament, but the principle still stands: questions are a great way to get to the heart of a Muslim. We need to ask questions such as: "What is most important for you in life?" or "What do you believe about Jesus?" or "How can we be most pleasing to God?" or "How can we deserve to be in heaven for eternity?"

When it comes time to share the gospel with our Muslim friends, it is best to look for bridges from their life to the gospel. In Acts 17, when Paul proclaims the gospel to the Athenian philosophers at the Areopagus, he uses an inscription to an unknown God that was found on one of their objects of worship as a bridge to the gospel. He also used the poetry of their culture to point them to One who is not created by hands but is to be worshipped by all. As God brings needs in your Muslim neighbor's life to your attention, you can share how God met those needs in your own life.

I have found bridges to the gospel in the most trivial of ways. On a recent trip to Athens, I found myself sharing the gospel with a man from Afghanistan who was there after fleeing from the Taliban. The man's name was Noor, which in the Farsi language means "light." I was able to use his name as a bridge to talk about Jesus, the light of the world that shines in the darkness (John 3:19–21). I told him that evil men hate the light and hide from it because they love their evil deeds. He nodded, as he had just seen the evil of the Taliban in his own life. I told him that the enemy of God is busy blinding the eyes of unbelievers from seeing the light of the gospel of Jesus, but that I was praying that God would shine in his heart the light of the knowledge of the gospel of Christ (2 Cor 4:4–6). I then told him that if he turns to Jesus, he will receive life and become one of God's people to declare to the world the excellencies of the One who called him out of darkness and into his marvelous light (1 Pet 2:9).

In sharing the gospel, we need to be clear to point Muslims to the only way that they can find life and freedom from sin: by grace through faith in Christ. They need to see that God has made one way for us to be saved from our sins and for him to receive the glory for it, and that is through the finished work of Jesus Christ on the cross, dying in our place the death that we deserved to pay for our sins.

I once was asked by a Muslim if I knew with complete certainty that I would be in heaven. When I told him that I did, he called my declaration the most arrogant thing. I told him it is completely arrogant to believe that I will be in heaven based on what I have done, but there is no arrogance (in fact, it requires humility) in saying I will be in heaven based solely on what Christ has done for me.

Today I am a pastor of Providence Church in Frisco, Texas, and I frequently equip Iranian pastors overseas who are planting churches in the Muslim world. I am humbled that I get to know Christ and be a part of making him known. There is no way I would be in this place if it had not been for a second-grade tutor who was determined to invest in my life. I believe there are many more Muslims like me in your community. I pray that you will be obedient to Jesus as he calls you to invest in the life of a Muslim in your path for the sake of the gospel!

Reflection Questions

1. What aspect of the Islamic faith (view of man, view of Jesus, etc.) should you address first when evangelizing Muslims?
2. How does a Christian's view of good works compare with a Muslim's?
3. What are specific ways you can pray for Muslims to come to know Christ?
4. What are some ways you can share the love of Christ with Muslims both in word and in deed?

AFTERWORD

A BIBLICAL-THEOLOGICAL FRAMEWORK FOR UNDERSTANDING IMMIGRATION

Miguel Echevarria

Imagine yourself at a perfectly boring dinner party. Everyone is standing around exchanging pleasantries, trying to be friendly.[1] You, of course, are well versed on the latest political news and are itching to strike up a lively conversation. So you decide to bring up a topic that will send tempers flaring and has the power to instigate marches and protests: immigration. After lighting the match, you stand back and watch the place go up in flames.

While saying this tongue-in-cheek, I do believe my sarcasm reflects the sad reality that immigration is one of the most contentious topics in America. Even a person with minimal access to social media and cable news can affirm that our news outlets dedicate considerable time to reporting about sanctuary cities, building a wall, immigration bans, and deportations. Each source provides their

---

[1] This essay is a revised version of an article ("Theology: A Biblical Perspective on Immigration") that I contributed to Alan Cross, *Preaching God's Heart for Immigrants and Refugees: Reaching the Nations in North America*, a resource that was distributed at the 2017 Southern Baptist Convention in Phoenix, Arizona.

own politicized perspective on immigration, often vilifying anyone who disagrees. Lost in the hostility are the objects of these discussions—people we call "foreigners," "immigrants," or "illegals." Human beings created in God's image, most of whom are not gun-toting, drug-smuggling criminals; they are just people trying to support their families.

Unfortunately, even Christian views on immigration tend to reflect political ideologies and America's toxic news culture.[2] Of all people, Christians should allow the Bible, versus their nationalistic identities and political parties, to shape their view of the stranger. I am not saying that we should be ashamed to be Americans, or that we should stop supporting political parties. What I am saying is that we have a duty to honor Jesus over a flag or a donkey or an elephant. If we look to the Scriptures before running to our favorite news anchor's podcast, we will see that God's people have historically been called "immigrants." That's right—you and me and all people from every tribe, tongue, and nation who follow Jesus. We are all a bunch of immigrants looking for a better home. We may be very comfortable in America, but this is not where we belong. We seek a better place—one where a crucified, olive-skinned, Middle Eastern man will reign as King. And one more thing: as immigrants in the present world, we are to love the sojourner in our midst—regardless of legal status. Scripture is very clear on this.

Now that I have ruffled some feathers, let me turn to Scripture. I will make this point by examining the theme of immigration in the Old Testament. Then I will examine this theme in the New Testament, focusing on 1 Peter. Lastly, I will address 1 Pet 2:13–17 and Rom 13:1–7, two passages that Christians often use as open-and-shut cases against caring for immigrants.

---

[2] A recent LifeWay Research survey, titled "Evangelical Views on Immigration," shows that the evangelical view of immigration is more influenced by the media than by the Bible. See chap. 8, n. 6.

While I do believe that immigration is a thread that runs throughout the storyline of Scripture, this essay will only give us a glimpse of this central theme. A more comprehensive work is warranted. For now, my hope is that this essay might begin to shape our biblical-theological framework for thinking through the topic of immigration—so that instead of running to cable news and social media, we might consider the Bible's story about a group of chosen exiles looking for a better existence.

Old Testament

Early in the Genesis narrative, we see that God makes a covenant with a pagan named Abraham (Genesis 12, 15), promising him land, offspring, and blessing. The land promise sets Abraham and his descendants, Isaac (Genesis 35, 37) and Jacob (Genesis 28, 32), on a migration to Canaan. Along the way, Abraham's descendants become slaves in Egypt for 400–430 years (Exodus 1–14). To put it lightly, they were poorly treated immigrants. Yet hardship was part of God's plan for Israel.

When God makes a covenant with Abraham, he foreknows those sojourners' time in Egypt, assuring Abraham that his offspring would be aliens—unwelcome and detestable ones at that—in a foreign land (Gen 15:13). The status of "immigrant" would be a common one for Israel in the Old Testament, so much so that the biblical authors frequently use the word *gare* to refer to God's people.[3] Most translations render this term as "sojourner," "stranger," or "alien." The translation "immigrant," however, more precisely communicates the

[3] Ludwig Koehler and Walter Baumgartner, *The Hebrew and Aramaic Lexicon of the Old Testament*, vol. 1, trans. and ed. M. E. J. Richardson (Leiden: Brill, 1995), 201, note that גֵּר often refers to "a man who (along with his family) leaves a village and tribe because of war . . . famine . . . epidemic, blood guilt, etc. and seeks shelter in residence at another place, where his right of landed property, marriage and taking part in jurisdiction, cult and war has been curtailed."

reality of the old-covenant community as they wander from one place to the next (Gen 15:13).[4]

After God delivers them from Egypt, the Israelites resume their migration. As they are sojourning, God gives his people the law (Exodus 20), within which God displays his love and concern for the immigrant. He requires the Israelites to treat foreigners with love and kindness, contrary to the way they were treated in Egypt (Exod 22:21; Deut 23:7). The law did not stipulate qualifications for such treatment, such as a green card or a work visa.[5] God's people were to love and care for the immigrant as they would other vulnerable persons, such as the fatherless and the widow (Deut 10:18). Moreover, the law gave strangers the same social protections as native Israelites (Lev 19:34). They were entitled, for example, to fair treatment as laborers (Deut 24:14) and rest from work on the Sabbath (Exod 20:10). Of course, the history of Israel underscores that the nation did not heed the law; the people wronged, abused, and mistreated immigrants. The prophets raged against Israel's treatment of the foreigner (Ezek 22:7–9; Mal 3:5). Israel's flagrant abuse of the immigrant was one of the primary reasons they were eventually sent into exile.

While Christians may not be the nation of Israel, loving the immigrant is a principle that applies to all believers. We see this clearly as both Leviticus 19 and Matthew 22 exhort love of neighbor. To be perfectly clear, an undocumented person *is* your neighbor. Also, the parable of the good Samaritan in Luke 10 shows that we are to love and care for the needs of those of different ethnicities, even groups against whom we have strong enmity. Unfortunately, as

---

[4] Tim Keller makes this point in his *Generous Justice: How God's Grace Makes Us Just* (New York: Riverhead, 2010).

[5] I am not saying that strangers were granted all the rights and privileges as Israelites. Exodus 12:48, for example, requires that foreigners be circumcised before partaking in the Passover. My argument focuses on the fact that foreigners were granted the same "social protections" as native Israelites.

Christians, we are more like the priest and the Levite in Luke 10 than the Samaritan.

In view of the Samaritan's kindness, Jesus's closing words in this parable are especially important today: "Go and do likewise" (v. 37 NIV). What if Christians heeded these words; that is, to be a neighbor to the vulnerable? Would that not lead to a more empathetic view of the immigrant? Would that not lead to more gospel fruit among sojourners, viewing them as people in need of redemption, or fellow brothers and sisters in Christ, rather than as nuisances and threats?[6]

Since the Israelites did not heed the exhortation to love the stranger, God sent them into exile, centuries after entering the land (Kings–Chronicles). Once again, the Israelites became immigrants under the rule of foreign nations, such as Babylon and Assyria. While some scholars argue that the Israelites returned to the land in Ezra, chapter 9 clearly affirms that God's people were slaves under a foreign ruler.[7] They, therefore, longed for the day when they would be home. But they did not expect to return to one strip of territory (i.e., Canaan); their expectation was eschatological. They expected

---

[6] I have not even mentioned anything related to wages and time off for immigrants. I am just trying to scratch the surface on a very deep problem. That is, we treat immigrants far worse than we treat American citizens, not granting them the same protections that we grant citizens. The Old Testament cries out against such practices (Exod 20:10; Deut 24:14).

[7] N. T. Wright, *Paul and the Faithfulness of God* (Minneapolis: Fortress, 2013), 1:151, points out that "both Ezra and Nehemiah, in their great prayers, very similar to Daniel 9, speak of a continuing state which is hardly the great liberation the prophets had promised." Stephen Dempster, *Dominion and Dynasty: A Theology of the Hebrew Bible*, New Studies in Biblical Theology 15 (Downers Grove: InterVarsity, 2003), 224, contends that since a change of heart has not occurred in the people, "exile continues even though Israel is in the land." Thus, Israel anticipates a future redemption. At best, the return in Ezra is a type of the eschatological return that will occur at the Parousia. At that time, Christ will reign over his people, granting them the peace and prosperity for which they have longed (Ezekiel 36–37; Isaiah 65–66; Revelation 20–22).

to inherit a reconstituted earth (Psalms 2; Ezekiel 36–37; Isaiah 65–66). The Old Testament ends with this expectation that one day things would be "very good" again (as in Gen 1:31), anticipating the day when God's people would no longer be immigrants.

The New Testament authors had this Old Testament story in mind as they wrote their letters—a story that reaches its climax and culmination in Jesus the Messiah, who will deliver his people from exile and into a new earth.[8] Of these letters, Peter's first epistle is especially relevant for a discussion of immigration, for he takes the label "immigrant" and applies it to dispersed Christians throughout the Roman Empire.

1 Peter

Peter wasted no time in alerting his readers to their present reality, calling them elect immigrants (1 Pet 1:1).[9] Later, he calls them

---

[8] Some, such as Rudolf Bultmann, give little priority to the Old Testament as the foundational element of the thought of the New Testament authors. See his *Theology of the New Testament* (New York: Scribner's, 1951; repr., Waco: Baylor, 2007). Regarding Paul, Richard Hays, *Echoes of Scripture in the Letters of Paul* (New Haven: Yale, 1989), rightly argues that "we will have great difficulty understanding Paul, the pious first century Jew, unless we seek to situate his discourse appropriately within what . . . enveloped him: Scripture." The same is true of other New Testament authors, such as Peter. A prime example of Peter's thinking is found in Acts 2, where he argues that Jesus is the climax of Old Testament (Jewish) history. To rightly understand the New Testament, we must see that it continues and fulfills the story of the Old Testament.

[9] Henry George Liddell and Robert Scott, *A Greek-English Lexicon*, 9th ed., rev. Henry Stuart Jones (Oxford: Clarendon Press, 1996), 1337, translate παρεπίδημος as one "sojourning in a strange place." Walter Bauer, *A Greek Lexicon of the New Testament and Other Early Christian Literature*, 3rd. ed., rev. and ed. Fredrick William Danker (Chicago: University of Chicago Press, 2001), 775, renders the word similarly and notes that "the author of 1 Pt makes an intimate connection between the status of the addressees (as virtual visitors in the world because of their special relation to God through Jesus Christ) and

immigrants and sojourners (2:11). These terms are often used to refer to someone who is living in a foreign land, either by force or by his or her own volition.[10] Peter uses them to underscore that Christians are living as immigrants in the present world, awaiting entrance into the place where their citizenship truly lies (1:4; 2 Peter 3). Rome is not their home. They are citizens of an eschatological realm where Jesus is King. Thus, they are a strange people, for their allegiance to Jesus necessitates that they abstain from the sinful behavior of the citizens of the present world (1 Pet 4:4), making them subject to persecution (4:12).

On a macro level, the scattered Jewish exiles in the prophetic corpus share the same hope with new-covenant believers. That is, they are exiles in the present cosmos, awaiting the inheritance of a new creation (Isaiah 65–66; Romans 4, 8; Revelation 21–22). This is the story of God's multiethnic people, who will be saved through the Messiah. Thus, an overarching view of the canon makes clear that God's people have historically been strangers. Paul even takes the vocabulary of sojourner and stranger and applies it to the former life of Gentiles (all nonethnic Jews): they were strangers before becoming citizens of the household of God (Eph 2:19).

What does this all mean for present-day Christians? Again, I will be blunt: we are immigrants—you and me, all of us. Though we may feel very comfortable in the United States, this is not our home. Our primary citizenship is not associated with our present geographical borders. The New Testament teaches that all Christians—regardless of socioeconomic status, color of skin, or legal standing—hold

their moral responsibility." Rather than "sojourner," in 1 Pet 1:1 I have chosen to translate παρεπίδημος as "immigrant," for it accurately communicates the status of Peter's audience, in that they are "immigrants" in this strange world, migrating to the future world promised to them.

[10] See W. Grundmann, "παρεπίδημος," in *Theological Dictionary of the New Testament*, vol. 2, ed. Gerhard Kittel, trans. G. W. Bromiley (Grand Rapids: Eerdmans, 1964), 64–65; K. L. and M. A. Schmidt, "πάροικος," in *TDNT*, 5:842–53.

the status of "immigrant." We are a peculiar people, citizens of a land with a set of values and commitments distinct from the one in which we presently live.

Peter's letter should, therefore, raise some questions regarding the way we think about immigration. Do we primarily see ourselves as immigrants in the present world? Or do we mainly think of ourselves as citizens of our present nation, prioritizing our citizenship in America over our citizenship in a new creation? Do we realize that we have more in common with Christian immigrants from Syria or Mexico, regardless of legal status, than with unbelieving Americans or secular members of our respective political parties? Do we understand that members of our Christian family—people with whom we will stand before the throne of Christ—are from ethnic groups outside of the United States, many of whom have come to this country without prerequisite paperwork and may be returned to places where they will be placed in harm's way, such as the Middle East? It would be highly unlikely that we would take such an ambivalent stance if the legal status of a flesh-and-blood relative were at stake. People would call us callous and inhuman, having no regard for family.

In view of Scripture, I cannot conclude anything other than that our primary familial allegiance should be to the kingdom that has yet to be fully revealed, one that comprises people from all nationalities over our loyalty to America. Does not Jesus indicate the same (Mark 10:29–30; Luke 14:26)?

But I know that I may still need to convince you. After all, do we not have laws? Are we not called to obey such laws regarding immigration? How then are we to love and care for a person who may be here illegally—thus breaking our civil law—even if he is a brother in Christ?

Christians use two passages, 1 Pet 2:13–17 and Rom 13:1–7, as open-and-shut cases for obeying immigration laws and denying help to the sojourner.[11] I will now take a brief look at these texts.

---

[11] See M. Daniel Carroll R., *Christians at the Border: Immigration, the Church, and the Bible*, 2nd ed. (Grand Rapids: Brazos, 2013), 121–26.

1 Peter 2:13–17 and Romans 13:1–7

In the very letter in which he calls Christians strangers and immigrants, Peter also calls believers to be subject to governing authorities (1 Pet 2:13–17). Contrary to what some may assume, Peter is not exhorting Christians to blindly obey the government, for governments may demand that citizens obey sinful decrees. Thomas Schreiner insightfully argues:

> [Christians] obey the injunctions of governing authorities ultimately because of their reverence and submission for the Lord. We have an implication here that ruling authorities should be resisted if commands were issued that violated the Lord's will. It is impossible to imagine that one would obey commands that contravened God's dictates "for the Lord's sake."[12]

I heartily agree with Schreiner's reading of 1 Pet 2:13–17. Consequently, Christians only submit to laws that both agree with and do not conflict with God's will in the Bible. We can also read similarly Paul's parallel exhortation to submit to God-ordained authorities in Rom 13:1–7. Such human authorities are fallible and can err. Christians, therefore, have a duty to examine laws in light of Scripture before yielding to a government's demands. Blind obedience is never an option.

Historically, Christians have not followed governments into sin. Consider the past couple of centuries. Have Christians not resisted, and even protested, submission to laws regarding slavery and segregation? Have Christians not actively campaigned against laws regarding abortion and same-sex marriage? Consequently, then, do we not also have a duty to examine immigration laws in view of Scripture? If we have never thought of doing so, have we simply assumed that our

---

[12] Thomas Schreiner, *1, 2 Peter, Jude*, New American Commentary (Nashville: Holman, 2003), 37:128.

immigration laws are just? An examination of American history may eliminate that presupposition.

At the very least, we should consider whether our immigration laws are in line with how God calls his people to treat the sojourner. We need, as M. Daniel Carroll R. proposes, "discerning submission, not blind obedience"[13]—for 1 Pet 2:13–17 and Rom 13:1–7 are not calls to follow governments blindly, nor are they open-and-shut cases against immigration. These passages are, instead, serious calls to obey civil authorities, but only in matters that are in obedience to God. Immigration, in my opinion, is an issue that we must examine closely before obeying the policies that any given administration decrees. As with all things, we must allow our minds to be renewed by God's Word, not by some unholy proclamation made by Caesar—and certainly not by someone yelling at a political convention, or some polarized news source.

Conclusion

In this essay, I have provided an overview of what the Bible says about immigration. Throughout the biblical narrative, God's singular, multiethnic people have been described as immigrants seeking a restored homeland. This diverse group finds their unity in their allegiance to Messiah, not in their present geographical boundaries. In other words, our allegiance to Christ takes precedence over our allegiance to America; our obedience to his inerrant word over America's error-prone legal code. And when the latter conflicts with the former, we have a duty to dissent peaceably. I have argued that this also applies to the government's policies on immigration.

I would like, then, to reiterate a key point: the United States of America is not our home. Christians in America, along with people from every tribe and tongue, are immigrants, strangers seeking a

[13] Carroll, *Christians at the Border*, 125.

restored inheritance. For this and many other reasons, we must love the stranger, for he may be a fellow Christian, sojourning to the same eternal destination. So, we have more in common with an undocumented Christian (as a fellow citizen of the heavenly kingdom) than with our American friend who shares the same political ideology but sleeps in on Sundays. Even if an immigrant is not a Christian, we are still called to love and care for him. Perhaps God might be so kind as to use our witness to win him over to Christ. Is that not more important than preserving our way of life? Is that not more important than spending time and energy on keeping out *bad hombres*? If we gave priority to the Bible, not to an elephant or a donkey, would we not spend less time talking about building a wall and more time building bridges to care for the immigrant? I heartily believe so.

EDITORS AND CONTRIBUTORS

Editors:

Micah Fries
Senior Pastor
Brainerd Baptist Church, Chattanooga, TN

Keith S. Whitfield
Associate Professor of Theology
Dean of Graduate Studies
Vice President for Academic Administration
Southeastern Baptist Theological Seminary

Contributors:

Bart Barber
Pastor
First Baptist Church, Farmersville, TX

Miguel Echevarria
Assistant Professor of New Testament and Greek
Director of Hispanic Leadership Development
Southeastern Baptist Theological Seminary

D. A. Horton
Pastor
Reach Fellowship, North Long Beach, CA
Chief Evangelist, Urban Youth Workers Institute

Ant Greenham
Associate Professor of Missions and Islamic Studies
Southeastern Baptist Theological Seminary

Ayman Ibrahim
Bill and Connie Jenkins Associate Professor of Islamic Studies
Director, Jenkins Center for the Christian Understanding of Islam
The Southern Baptist Theological Seminary

Steve A. Johnson
Assistant Professor of Ministry Care
Columbia International University

C. Fyne Nsofor
Associate Professor of Intercultural Studies
California Baptist University

Bob Roberts
Senior Pastor
Northwood Church, Keller, TX

Kambiz Saghaey
Coordinator for Persian Leadership Development
Southeastern Baptist Theological Seminary

Ed Stetzer
Billy Graham Chair of Church, Mission, and Evangelism
Director, Billy Graham Center; and Dean of the new School of Mission, Ministry, and Leadership
Wheaton College

Shirin Taber
Founder
Middle East Women's Leadership Network

Afshin Ziafat
Lead Pastor
Providence Church, Frisco TX

SUBJECT INDEX

G

H

I

J

M

N

O

P

Q

R

S

T

U

V

W

SCRIPTURE INDEX